Khomeinism

Khomeinism

*Essays on the
Islamic Republic*

Ervand Abrahamian

UNIVERSITY OF CALIFORNIA PRESS
BERKELEY LOS ANGELES LONDON

University of California Press
Berkeley and Los Angeles, California

University of California Press, Ltd.
London, England

© 1993 by
The Regents of the University of California

Library of Congress Cataloging-in-Publication Data

Abrahamian, Ervand, 1940–
    Khomeinism : essays on the Islamic Republic /
Ervand Abrahamian.
        p.   cm.
    Includes bibliographical references and index.
    ISBN 0-520-08173-0 (alk. paper).
    ISBN 0-520-08351-2 (pbk. : alk. paper)
    1. Iran—Politics and government—1979–
    2. Khomeini, Ruhollah.
    I. Title.
    DS318.8.A286 1993
    955.05′4—dc20
                                            92-39849
                                            CIP

Printed in the United States of America

For Shahen

Contents

Illustrations

Plates

Figures

Acknowledgments

I would like to thank the Social Science Research Council, the National Endowment for the Humanities, and Baruch College of the City University of New York for fellowships in 1989–91 to carry out the research for this book. I would also like to thank Shahen Abrahamian, Mohammad Reza Afshari, Sharough Akhavi, Abbas Amanat, Ali Gheissari, Ali Ashtiyani Mirsepasi, and Molly Nolan for reading and commenting on sections of the manuscript. Of course, they are in no way responsible for opinions or mistakes found in these pages.

Introduction

The life of Ayatollah Khomeini was so
shadowy, so overlain with myth and rumor,
that there was a lingering disagreement or
uncertainty about his ancestry, his true name
and his date of birth. But when he returned in
triumph on February 1, 1979—after 15 years
of exile—the old man left little doubt who he
was, or what he wanted for his ancient land.
. . . [H]e was inflexibly bent on expanding his
brand of revolutionary fundamentalism across
the Arab world.

Ayatollah Khomeini's obituary,
New York Times, *4 June 1989*

Perceptions of Khomeini

The stern image of Ayatollah Khomeini struck the consciousness
of the West much like the grade-B horror movies that appear on
American screens early each summer. Sinister and alien looking,
he at first aroused awe, fascination, and consternation. But when
the season was over, his bearded image had become blurred and
easily confused with competing horror shows. And now, more
than a decade later, the West associates his name, when it cares
to remember him, with "fanaticism," "radicalism," and, most
prevalent of all, "religious fundamentalism." Western journalists
consider him synonymous with religious atavism and search for
similar figures in such far-afield places as Israel, Nigeria, and
Indonesia.

1

It is not hard to fathom why the fundamentalist label has gained such wide currency. For conservatives, the term is associated with xenophobia, militancy, and radicalism. For liberals, it means extremism, fanaticism, and traditionalism. For radicals, it evokes theological obscurantism, political atavism, and the rejection of science, history, modernity, the Enlightenment, and the Industrial Revolution. Meanwhile, for Orientalists—still a big influence in Middle Eastern studies—the term is useful precisely because it implies that the Muslim world is intrinsically timeless, unchanging, irrational, backward looking, and programmed merely to replay old scripts from the time of the Prophet, the early caliphate, and the medieval Crusades. Typically, the *New York Times,* in reviewing the most influential book that portrays Khomeini as a clerical atavist, praised the work as a "major contribution" and thanked the author for showing how in the "mystifying" Iranian revolution the people rose up to "demand less freedom and fewer material things."[1] When the subject matter did not behave as expected, the same author coined the term "pragmatic fundamentalism"—an oxymoron if there ever was one.[2]

The central thesis of this book is that "populism" is a more apt term for describing Khomeini, his ideas, and his movement because this term is associated with ideological adaptability and intellectual flexibility, with political protests against the established order, and with socioeconomic issues that fuel mass opposition to the status quo. The label "fundamentalism," in contrast, implies religious inflexibility, intellectual purity, political traditionalism, even social conservatism, and the centrality of scriptural-doctrinal principles. "Fundamentalism" implies the rejection of the modern world; "populism" connotes attempts made by nation-states to enter that world.

There is more at issue here than semantics. On the one hand, if Khomeinism is a form of fundamentalism, then the whole movement is inherently incapable of adapting to the modern age and is trapped in an ideological closed circuit. On the other hand, if Khomeinism is a form of populism, it contains the potential for change and acceptance of modernity—even eventually of political pluralism, gender equality, individual rights, and social democracy. In arguing against the term "fundamentalism," I do not deny its existence in other countries or even among some Khomeini supporters in Iran. Nor do I deny the importance of religion to Khomeini himself. My argument is that Khomeinism should be seen as a flexible political movement expressing socio-economic grievances, not simply as a religious crusade obsessed with scriptural texts, spiritual purity, and theological dogma.

Each of the five chapters of this book elaborates on this central theme. Chapter 1 describes how Khomeini broke sharply with Shii traditions, borrowed radical rhetoric from foreign sources, including Marxism, and presented a bold appeal to the public based not on theological themes but on real economic, social, and political grievances. In short, he transformed Shiism from a conservative quietist faith into a militant political ideology that challenged both the imperial powers and the country's upper class. The final product has more in common with Third World populism—especially that of Latin America—than with conventional Shiism.[3]

Chapter 2 analyzes Khomeini's perceptions of private property, society, and the state. It describes how he adopted radical themes, inflamed social antagonisms, promised to redistribute wealth, and appealed blatantly to class sentiments—sentiments that some social scientists insist do not exist in Iran. At times he sounded more radical than the Marxists. But while adopting radical themes, he remained staunchly committed to the preservation of middle-class property. This form of middle-class radicalism again made him akin to Latin American populists, especially the Peronists.

Chapter 3 explores why the Islamic Republic celebrates May Day. It describes how the Khomeinists, while claiming to reject the West, have adopted International Workers' Day despite the fact that its themes, symbols, and language are all rooted in the traditions of European socialism. The meshing of religion and politics, of Islam and socialistic themes, can be seen every year in this annual celebration. These celebrations can also be used to measure how the regime has toned down its populistic rhetoric over the decade. In short, the unfolding of the Iranian Thermidor can be seen every year on May Day.

Chapter 4 looks at the Islamic Republic's treatment of Iranian history. It argues that the regime has systematically manipulated history through televised "recantations," newspapers, postage stamps, and school textbooks to bolster the clergy's reputation both as the long-time champions of the downtrodden masses against the rich and as the defenders of the nation against foreign powers. In other words, the Islamic Republic, like other ideologically charged states in the contemporary world, has used and abused history in an effort to win the "hearts and minds" of the general population.

Chapter 5 describes the paranoia prevalent throughout the political spectrum in Iran—among royalists and leftists as well as Khomeinists. It argues that the age of imperialism, as well as the traditional gap between state and society, has created the widespread notion that political actors on the Iranian stage are mere puppets manipulated from behind the scene *(posht-e pardeh)*. To qualify as an intelligent analyst, one is expected to ignore the stage distractions and instead detect the invisible hands. According to Khomeini, the imperial powers are constantly "plotting" *(tuteah)* to divide the population by means of "spies" *(jasouz-ha)*, "servants" *(nokar-ha)*, "dependents" *(vabasteh-ha)*, "traitors" *(khain-ha)*, and "fifth columnists" *(sotune-e panjom)*. The nation, thus, needs to be ever viligant against external conspirators and their internal agents. In this, as in many other aspects, Khomeini is strikingly similar to populists elsewhere.

These five analyses do not, of course, exhaust all aspects of Khomeinism. They skim over such important issues as women, religious and linguistic minorities, civil society, individual liberties, school curriculum, and due process of law. But an investigation of these topics would, I am sure, also reveal that the behavior of Khomeini and the Islamic Republic has been determined less by scriptural principles than by immediate political, social, and economic needs. The more we dig under the surface, the less we find of fundamentalism and the more of pragmatic—even opportunistic—populism. To analyze Khomeini's ideas, I have avoided secondary sources, relying as much as possible on his own works. Although rarely used by Western authors, these works are readily available in Persian.[4]

Khomeini's Life and Writings

The Islamic Republic has done its very best to portray Ayatollah Khomeini as the quintessential "man of the people." He is depicted as having been born into a humble family; losing his father in infancy, like the Prophet Mohammad; rising meteorically through the clerical hierarchy purely because of his scholastic abilities; devoting his whole adult life to the struggle against the Pahlavi tyrants; and leaving behind for his surviving son only one worldly possession—a family prayer rug. The truth is somewhat more complicated.

Ruhollah Khomeini was born in 1902 into a well-to-do family in Khomein, a small town located between Qom and Dezful, Arak, and Khonsar.[5] Both parents came from landed and clerical families well known in central Iran. His mother (who died in 1917) was the sister of a local landlord and the daughter of Akhund Hajj Mulla Hosayn Khonsari, a highly respected *mojtahed* (high-ranking cleric) in Isfahan. The Khonsaris monopolized the religious institutions of Arak and were related to Shaykh Fazlollah Nuri, the conservative *mojtahed* executed by the constitutional revolutionaries in 1909. Khomeini's father, Sayyid Mostafa (1861–1902), studied first in Isfahan with the Khonsari family and then in Najaf, in the Ottoman Empire, where he obtained his *ejtehad* (higher theology degree). Sayyid Mostafa had a retinue of servants and armed guards and used the title Fakhr al-Mojtahedin—it is not clear whether this was conferred on him by the monarch or was merely a title used by the local population.

Khomeini's paternal grandfather, Sayyid Ahmad, who died in 1868, was known as Hendi (the Indian), because he had been born in Kashmir, where his own father, originally from Nishapour, taught and traded under the name of Sayyid Din Ali Shah. Sayyid Ahmad studied in Najaf before laying down roots in Khomein in the 1830s. He bought land in the region and married the sister of a local notable. It is said that his future father-in-law, Yussef Khan, encouraged him to settle in the region so as to have another educated cleric in his domains. In the words of Khomeini's elder brother, Ayatollah Morteza Pasandideh, Sayyid Ahmad Hendi could well be described as "prosperous" since he kept an open house and owned substantial amounts of farmland in the nearby villages as well as a caravansary, fruit garden, and large house within Khomein.[6] Much of this was passed on to the grandchildren. Pasandideh, who appears to be highly status conscious, describes Yussef Khan as a local a^cyan (notable) with a retinue of servants and armed guards. The title *ayatollah* was not in current usage in the nineteenth century, but recent works use the term to refer to both Sayyid Ahmad and Sayyid Mostafa.[7] However, it seems that these two concentrated more on business ventures, leaving religious matters to the Khonsari side of the family.

In 1902, four months after Khomeini's birth, his father, Sayyid Mostafa, was ambushed and killed on the road to Arak. During the Islamic Revolution, much was made of this murder. Some claimed that he had been killed defending downtrodden peasants, and others that he had been assassinated by Reza Khan, the future Pahlavi shah of Iran. But Reza Khan at the time was no more than a Cossack cadet in Tehran, and the confrontation had arisen out of a family vendetta with the al-Ri^{c}yas, the other notable household in the locality. The al-Ri^{c}yas had imprisoned one of Sayyid Mostafa's men. Sayyid Mostafa had retaliated by imprisoning an al-Ri^{c}ya man, who had then died. The al-Ri^{c}yas took revenge by killing Sayyid Mostafa. According to Pasandideh, well-attended memorial services were held for him in Najaf, Isfahan, and Tehran, as well as in Khomein, Arak, and Golpayegan.

To obtain justice, Sayyid Mostafa's widow traveled to Tehran and, after lobbying there for three years, mainly through a leading court minister, succeeded in getting the shah to execute one of the assassins. He was publicly hanged and his head was displayed in the main bazaar. After the execution, she returned to Khomein, where she had left her infant son in the care of a wet nurse. Pasandideh writes that Khomeini was extremely fond of his nurse. Khomeini's mother died when he was fifteen.

Khomeini received much of his early education in his home town. He went first to a local *maktab* school, which received funds from his family, and then studied calligraphy, Arabic, and Persian literature with older relatives. In 1920, at the age of eighteen, he moved to Arak to study theology with the famous Shaykh

Abdul-Karim Ha'eri, a leading *marja^C-e taqlid* (a cleric of the highest rank). He was famous not only for his learning but also for his scrupulous avoidance of politics—even during the turbulent 1910s. Ha'eri became Khomeini's chief mentor for the next sixteen years. Khomeini's stay in Arak, however, did not last long. A year later, Ha'eri, together with his students, moved to Qom to revive the Fayzieh, a decaying nineteenth-century seminary.

In the next decade, Qom became Iran's major scholastic center, in part because of Ha'eri, in part because clerical refugees from Iraq settled there, and in part because Reza Shah patronized the center to reward the clerical scholars there for staying out of politics. Qom remained conspicuously quiet for much of Reza Shah's reign—in contrast to other religious centers, such as Mashad, which periodically burst into open opposition against Reza Shah's secular reforms. Yahya Dawlatabadi, the historian and politician, wrote that Reza Shah supported Ha'eri to counter the growth of republicanism, communism, and other forms of radicalism.[8] The notion that Qom is an ancient scholastic center is an invented tradition, and the claim that it was the hotbed of resistance against Reza Shah is self-serving fiction.

In the 1920s, Khomeini studied not only with Ha'eri but also with the other leading clergymen of Qom: Mirza Mohammad Ali, Hajji Sayyid Mohammad Taqi Khonsari, Sayyid Ali Yasabi Kashani, and, most important of all, Mirza Mohammad Ali Shahabadi, a prominent authority on the controversial subject of mysticism *(^{C}erfan)*. His tutorials with Shahabadi lasted some six years. Mysticism was controversial for the simple reason that it claimed to link the true believer directly with God, thereby undermining the clerical establishment. Aga Mohammad Behbehani, a leading nineteenth-century *mojtahed*, had been so opposed to mysticism that he had been nicknamed the Sufi Killer *(sufi-kush)*.

In the 1930s, Khomeini joined the Fayzieh faculty and published commentaries on hadiths, ethics, and mysticism. These books, all in Arabic, are *Misbah al-Hidaya* (Book of guidance), *Shahar Do'ay al-Sahar* (Interpretation of the dawn prayer), *Shahar Arbe'en* (Hadith explanations), and *Adab al-Salat* (Prayer literature). Some were elaborations of Shahabadi's lecture notes on mysticism.[9] After the revolution, his notes from Shahabadi's tutorials on medieval mystic philosophers were published under the titles *Fasus al-Hakim* (Jewels of wisdom) and *Misbah al-Uns* (Lamp of intimacy). Also in these years, Khomeini composed mystical poems in Persian, which were published posthumously in a highly decorative volume entitled *Devan-e She^{c}r* (Collection of poems). One of these poems praised al-Hallaj, the famous medieval mystic executed for his beliefs, and argued that the divine truth would never be found in the mosques and the seminaries.

In 1929 Khomeini married Batul, the daughter of Hojjat al-Islam Saqafi, a well-connected Tehran cleric. She remained his one and only wife for the rest of his life. They had seven children, five of whom—two sons and three daughters—survived infancy. His sons, Mostafa and Ahmad, spent much of their adult lives working as his assistants. Mostafa, the elder, died during the early stages of the revolution, creating rumors that he had been murdered by the regime. Ahmad continued at his father's side until his father's death in 1989 and then took charge of collecting and publishing his writings. Khomeini's three daughters married into clerical and bazaari (merchant) families. When Reza Shah decreed that everyone should take family surnames, Khomeini chose Mostafavi but in later years signed himself Ruhollah al-Mosavi al-Khomeini. His elder brother chose the name Pasandideh—a Persian word; his younger brother picked Hendi.

In 1937 Ha'eri died, and his place was gradually filled by Ayatollah Mohammad Hosayn Borujerdi, another highly apolitical cleric with strong organizational abilities. He also enjoyed free access to the palace. In the 1940s, Borujerdi reached an unwritten agreement with the young Mohammad Reza Shah. The former agreed to support the monarchy and to silence his politically motivated colleagues; the latter promised to relax his father's secular policies and lift the prohibition against the veil. By the mid-1940s, Borujerdi was recognized as Iran's supreme *marja^c-e taqlid*—an honor that had not been conferred since the nineteenth century. For radical and even reform-minded Muslims, Borujerdi was the epitome of the archconservative cleric who bolstered the status quo while claiming to keep out of politics. In the words of one religious dissident, these conservative ayatollahs turned the clerical establishment into a pillar of the Pahlavi regime.[10]

Khomeini's relations with Borujerdi were extremely close—especially after Khomeini's daughter married into the latter's family. He served as Borujerdi's teaching assistant and personal secretary, at crucial times conveying confidential messages to the shah. Pasandideh writes that Borujerdi sought Khomeini's advice on most issues, including political ones.[11] A fellow seminary teacher recounts that Borujerdi was the only person he had seen Khomeini address in writing as *ayatollah-e ^{c}ozma* (grand ayatollah).[12] What is more, Khomeini, on the whole, followed Borujerdi's instructions to stay out of politics. One disciple admitted later that during the Borujerdi years Khomeini had concentrated on teaching.[13] Another claimed that Khomeini had had many political differences with Borujerdi but kept them to himself for the sake of "Islamic unity."[14]

In 1943, Khomeini entered politics briefly by publishing an unsigned tract titled *Kashf al-Asrar* (Secrets unveiled).[15] Under the guise of defending Shiism against Wahhabism, he attacked contemporary secularists, particularly Reza Shah, Shariat Sangalaji (a reform-minded cleric who had openly supported the previous monarch), and Ahmad Kasravi (the leading contemporary historian of Shiism and Iran). One of Kasravi's supporters, a lapsed cleric named Ali Akbar Hakimzadeh, had just published an explosive book titled *Asrar-e Hazar Saleh* (Thousand year secrets), in which he scrutinized the historical authenticity of the central Shii myths. *Kashf al-Asrar* was for the most part a response to it. Khomeini himself stated that he had taken a two-month leave of absence from teaching to write his response.[16] His own title may have been borrowed from *Kashf al-Ghita* (Obscurities unveiled), a famous nineteenth-century work defending the authority of the clergy from dissidents who claimed that the faithful could find the truth by going directly to the scriptures.

After this brief foray, Khomeini again withdrew from politics—even during the turbulent years of the oil crisis, when Ayatollah Abdul-Qasem Kashani, the main political cleric, broke Borujerdi's ban on political involvement and actively supported Premier

Mohammad Mosaddeq against the British. One disciple later boasted that Khomeini had not been enticed by Mosaddeq's "anti-regime and anti-imperialist propaganda."[17] Khomeini spent much of the 1950s teaching at the Fayzieh, helping Borujerdi administer the Qom endowments and working on his *Towzih al-Masa'el* (Questions clarified). (All senior clerics now needed to publish a significant work to establish their reputations as grand ayatollahs). It was published in 1961 in Arabic in Najaf.

Khomeini's real entry into politics came in 1962–63—soon after Borujerdi's death and the inauguration of a series of reforms later known as the White Revolution. These reforms were attacked by much of the religious establishment, including such grand ayatollahs as Mohammad Kazem Shariatmadari, Shahab al-Din Marashi-Najafi, Mohammad Reza Golpayegani, Ahmad Khonsari, and Mohammad Taqi Qomi. Khomeini's attack, however, focused not on land redistribution, the reform's central piece, but the new electoral law enfranchising women and the referendum itself endorsing the White Revolution.[18] According to Khomeini's proclamation, the electoral law was un-Islamic and the referendum unconstitutional—"no less so than Mosaddeq's 1953 referendum for dissolving Parliament."[19] These denunciations helped turn the June 1963 Moharram processions into violent street protests against the regime. Khomeinists date the beginning of their movement to the June Uprising (Qiyam-e Khordad). One prominent cleric has recently revealed that in the discussions preceding these protests, Khomeini insisted that the clergy stay clear of land reform on the grounds that if they denounced it the shah would be able to label them pro-landlord mullas.[20]

In the midst of the 1963 crisis, Khomeini was arrested and detained in Tehran for two months. On his release, the regime spread the rumor that he had agreed to stay out of state affairs because he believed that "politics by its very nature is dirty and demeaning." In 1964, however, Khomeini obtained the perfect opportunity to expose these rumors. Late in that year, the shah extended diplomatic immunity to American military advisers. Khomeini promptly compared this to the notorious nineteenth-century Capitulation Agreements, accusing the shah of betraying Iran and endangering Islam.[21] He was immediately rearrested. This time the regime was not willing to take chances and deported him to Turkey, from where he made his way to Najaf in Iraq. His deportation, as well as his anti-Capitulations attacks, established him as the leading antiregime ayatollah. Other ayatollahs complained; he denounced. Others compromised; he persisted in his denunciations.

Khomeini was to spend the next thirteen years in Najaf. In the first six years of exile, he concentrated on teaching religious jurisprudence (*fiqh*), not mysticism, and writing academic works, especially *Menasek Haj* (Pilgrimage rituals) and a five-part tome entitled *Ketab-e Bey^C* (Book of trade). His classes on law were so interesting that he often lectured past the assigned hour. "Others," writes one disciple, "were flabbergasted to hear that he could keep his audience's attention well past the one-hour class period."[22] In these years, he issued no more than fourteen political pronouncements.

In early 1970, Khomeini shook the religious establishment with a series of seventeen lectures denouncing the apolitical clergy as well as the whole institution of monarchy. It is thought that the target of his attack was Ayatollah Abul-Qasem Khoi, the eldest *mojtahed* in Najaf and the one most eager to continue the Ha'eri-Borujerdi tradition of keeping the faithful out of politics. These lectures, delivered in the main bazaar mosque in Najaf, were soon circulated in Iran under the title *Velayat-e Faqih: Hokumat-e Islami* (The jurist's guardianship: Islamic government). It became the main Khomeinist handbook. Some—embarrassed by its contents—claim that this edition is unreliable and that it is a poor translation of the original Arabic. But the original lectures were in Persian, and in fact Khomeini, like many Iranian senior clerics, never attained fluency in spoken Arabic.[23]

In subsequent years, Khomeini issued a constant stream of decrees, sermons, messages, interviews, and political pronouncements. By late 1978, when the revolution was in full swing, he was giving daily declarations and press interviews.[24] From 1979 until 1986—from his return to Iran until his health deteriorated—he gave weekly audiences and sermons.[25] Even after suffering a major heart attack in March 1986, he continued to write decrees, homilies, and exhortations, including a farewell message published immediately after his death in June 1989, *Matn-e Kamel-e Vasiyatnameh-e Elahi va Siyasi-ye Imam Khomeini* (The complete text of Imam Khomeini's divine will and political testament). It was later translated into English, Russian, Arabic, Turkish, and Urdu. These pronouncements contained little theology but had much to do with sociopolitical issues. Even his homilies revealed a good deal about his social attitudes. Intended for the public at large, they used simple language and were disseminated widely through the mass media, especially television. Khomeini's use of everyday language made him the butt of upper-class humor.

From 1962 until 1989, Khomeini issued more than 610 decrees, sermons, interviews, and political pronouncements. The Islamic Republic, under his son's guidance, has published many, but not all, of them in a seventeen-volume work entitled *Sahifah-e Nur: Majmu^{c}eh Rahnavard-ha-ye Imam Khomeini* (Leaves of illumination: Collection of Imam Khomeini's messages). It has also published selected quotations in twenty-two booklets with such titles as *Zan* (Women), *Shakhsiyat-ha* (Personalities), *Shahid va Shahadat* (Martyr and martyrdom), *Jang va Jahad* (War and crusade), *Enqelab-e Islami* (Islamic revolution), *Zed-e Enqelabi* (Counterrevolutionary), *Mardom, Ummat, Mellat* (People, community, nation), *Tarikh-e Iran* (Iranian history), *Azadi* (Freedom), *Goruha-ye Siyasi* (Political groups), *Este^{c}mar* (Imperialism), *Nahzat-ha-ye Azadibakhsh* (Liberation movements), and *Mostazafin, Mostakberin* (The oppressed and the oppressors).

The fact that the regime constantly reprints these booklets but not his theological works testifies to their political importance. Without them there would have been no Khomeinism. Without Khomeinism there would have been no revolution—at least, not the Islamic Revolution. And without the Islamic Revolution, Khomeini would have been no more than a footnote to Iranian history. This book, consequently, will analyze Khomeinism mainly—though not solely—through the original versions of these sermons, decrees, press interviews, and political declarations.

I

Fundamentalism or Populism?

> How did Ayatollah Ruhollah Khomeini become
> an imam? Much like the Holy Prophet
> Abraham: he carried out God's will, smashed
> idols, was willing to sacrifice his own son, rose
> up against tyrants, and led the oppressed
> against their oppressors.
>
> *A parliamentary deputy, Kayhan-e Hava'i,*
> *21 June 1989*

Introduction

The slippery label of fundamentalist has been thrown at Khomeini
so often that it has stuck—so much so that his own supporters in
Iran, finding no equivalent in Persian or Arabic, have proudly
coined a new word, *bonyadegar,* by translating literally the English term "fundamental-ist." This is especially ironic since the
same individuals never tire of denouncing their opponents as *elteqati* (eclectic) and *gharbzadeh* (contaminated with Western dis-
eases). Despite the widespread use of the label, I would like to
argue that the transference of a term invented by early twentieth-
century Protestants in North America to a political movement in
the contemporary Middle East is not only confusing but also misleading and even downright wrong, for the following reasons.

First, if fundamentalism means the acceptance of one's scriptural text as free of human error, then all Muslim believers would
have to be considered fundamentalists, for, after all, it is an essential article of Islam that the Koran is the absolute Word of God. By
this definition, all Middle Eastern politicians who have appealed to

13

Islam would have to be defined as fundamentalist: President Sadat of Egypt, King Hasan of Morocco, Saddam Hosayn of Iraq, Mohammad Reza Shah of Iran, not to mention the Muslim Brotherhood, the Wahhabis, the Iranian Mojahedin, and the Afghan Mojahedin.

Second, if the term implies that the believer can grasp the true meaning of the religion by going directly to the essential text, bypassing the clergy and their scholarship, then few Muslim theologians would qualify—Khomeini certainly would not be among the few. He would be the first to stress the importance of the Shii traditions and clerical scholarship. As a senior member of the Usuli School of Shiism, Khomeini opposed the Akhbari dissenters of the previous centuries, who had argued that believers could understand Islam by relying mainly on the Koran and the Shii imams. Khomeini, on the contrary, insisted that the Koran was too complex for the vast majority and that even Archangel Gabriel, who had brought the Koran to Mohammad, had not been able to understand the "inner meanings" of what he conveyed. Khomeini frequently argued that these "inner layers" could be grasped only by those who were familiar with Arabic, knew the teachings of the Twelve Shii Imams, had studied the ancient and contemporary works of the clerical scholars, and, most nebulous of all, had somehow been endowed with *^cerfan* (gnostic knowledge).[1] Only the most learned clerics who had reached the highest level of mystic consciousness could comprehend the true essence of Islam. In short, the Truth was not accessible to everyone, especially to the layperson.

Third, if fundamentalism means finding inspiration in a Golden Age of early Islam, then of course all believing Muslims would qualify. If it means striving to re-create this Golden Age, Khomeini by no means qualifies. It is true that in his earlier years he implied that Mohammad's Mecca and Imam Ali's caliphate were the models to replicate. But it is also true that in later years he argued that even the Prophet and Imam Ali had not been able to surmount the horrendous problems of their societies.[2] What is more, in the euphoria of revolutionary success, he boasted that the Islamic Republic of Iran had surpassed all previous Muslim societies, including that of the Prophet, in implementing true religion "in all spheres of life, particularly in the material and the spiritual spheres."[3] In short, the Islamic Republic of Iran had supplanted Mohammad's Mecca and Imam Ali's caliphate as the Muslim Golden Age. This claim no doubt raised eyebrows among real fundamentalists.

Fourth, if fundamentalism implies the rejection of the modern nation-state and contemporary state boundaries, then Khomeini does not qualify.[4] Although at times he claimed imperialism had divided the Islamic community *(ummat)* into rival states and nations, he both implicitly and explicitly accepted the existence of the territorial nation-state. He increasingly spoke of the Iranian fatherland, the Iranian nation, the Iranian patriot, and the honorable people of Iran. He even disqualified one of his staunch supporters from entering the 1980 presidential elections on the grounds that his father had been born in Afghanistan. The nationalistic language, together with the use of exclusively Shii symbols and imagery, helps explain why the Khomeinists have had limited success in exporting their revolution.

Fifth, if fundamentalism suggests the strict implementation of the laws and institutions found in the basic religious texts, then Khomeini again was no fundamentalist. Many of Khomeini's most rigid laws, including those concerning the veil, are found not in the Koran but in later traditions—some of them with non-Muslim antecedents. Similarly, the whole constitutional structure of the Islamic Republic was modeled less on the early caliphate than on de Gaulle's Fifth Republic. When parliamentary deputies questioned the Islamic precedents of some tax laws, Hojjat al-Islam Ali Akbar Hashemi Rafsanjani, one of Khomeini's closest disciples and the future president of the Islamic Republic, retorted in exasperation: "Where in Islamic history do you find Parliament, President, Prime Minister, and Cabinet of Ministers? In fact, eighty per cent of what we now do has no precedent in Islamic history."[5] Khomeini's break with tradition is glaringly obvious in a realm close to his own heart—that of Islamic law. Before the revolution, he categorically insisted that the sacred law *(shari^c a)* could be implemented only if the religious judges *(fuqaha)* were entirely

free of all state intervention, especially of the cumbersome judi-
cial-review process.[6] After the revolution, however, he found it
expedient to retain a centralized judicial structure, including an
elaborate review process, both to provide some semblance of
uniformity and to retain ultimate control over local judges.[7] In
fact, the new constitution guaranteed citizens the right of judicial
appeal.

Sixth, if fundamentalism means a dogmatic adherence to tradition and a rejection of modern society, then Khomeini does not
qualify. He frequently stressed that Muslims needed to import
such essentials as technology, industrial plants, and modern civilization *(tamaddon-e jadid)*. His closest disciples often mocked the
"traditionalists" *(sunnati)* for being "old-fashioned" *(kohanipe-
rast)*. They accused them of obsessing over ritual purity; prevent-
ing their daughters from going to school; insisting that young girls
should always be veiled, even when no men were present; denouncing such intellectual pursuits as art, music, and chess-play-
ing; and, worst of all, refusing to take advantage of newspapers,
electricity, cars, airplanes, telephones, radios, and televisions.[8] In
the words of Hojjat al-Islam Mohammad Javad Hojjati-Kermani,
another Khomeini disciple: "These traditionalists should be labeled reactionary [*ertejayi*] for they want us to return to the age
of the donkey. What we need is not the worship of the past but a
genuine *renasans* [literal transliteration of the word 'Renais-
sance']."[9] The concepts, not to mention the terminology, make
mockery of the Orientalist claim that Khomeinism is merely another recurrence of the old traditionalist "epidemic" that has
plagued Islam from its very early days.[10]

Seventh, the term "fundamentalism," because of its origins in
early twentieth-century American Protestantism, has distinct conservative political connotations. American fundamentalists, react-
ing against contemporary "social gospel" preachers, argued that
the goal of true religion was not to change society but to "save
souls" by preserving the literal interpretation of the Bible—especially on such doctrinal issues as Creation, Judgment Day, and the
Virgin Birth. Khomeinism, in contrast, while by no means oblivi-
ous to doctrinal matters, is predominantly and primarily concerned with sociopolitical issues—with revolution against the roy-

alist elite, expulsion of the Western imperialists, and mobilization of what it terms the *mostazafin* (oppressed) against the *mostakberin* (oppressors). In fact, Khomeini succeeded in gaining power mainly because his public pronouncements carefully avoided esoteric doctrinal issues. Instead, they hammered away at the regime on its most visible political, social, and economic shortcomings.

Finally, the term "fundamentalist" conjures up the image of inflexible orthodoxy, strict adherence to tradition, and rejection of intellectual novelty, especially from outside. In the political arena, however, Khomeini, despite his own denials, was highly flexible, remarkably innovative, and cavalier toward hallowed traditions. He is important precisely because he discarded many Shii concepts and borrowed ideas, words, and slogans from the non-Muslim world. In doing so, he formulated a brand-new Shii interpretation of state and society. The final product has less in common with conventional fundamentalism than with Third World populism, especially in Latin America.

The term "populism" needs some elaboration. By it I mean a movement of the propertied middle class that mobilizes the lower classes, especially the urban poor, with radical rhetoric directed against imperialism, foreign capitalism, and the political establishment. In mobilizing the "common people," populist movements use charismatic figures and symbols, imagery, and language that have potent value in the mass culture. Populist movements promise to drastically raise the standard of living and make the country fully independent of outside powers. Even more important, in attacking the status quo with radical rhetoric, they intentionally stop short of threatening the petty bourgeoisie and the whole principle of private property. Populist movements, thus, inevitably emphasize the importance, not of economic-social revolution, but of cultural, national, and political reconstruction.

Khomeini's View of the State

Throughout the Middle Ages the Shii clergy, unlike their Sunni counterparts, failed to develop a consistent theory of the state. The Sunnis, recognizing the Umayyad and Abbasid caliphs as the

Prophet's legitimate successors, accepted the reigning monarchs as lawful as long as these rulers did not blatantly violate Islamic norms. Had not the Prophet himself said, "My community will never agree on an error"? Had not the Koran commanded, "Obey God, His Prophet, and those among you who have authority"? Had not al-Ghazzali, the prominent medieval philosopher, argued that rulers were appointed by God, that rebellion against them was tantamount to rejection of the Almighty, and that forty years of tyranny were better than one single day of anarchy? Following these leads, the Sunni clergy associated political obedience with religious duty and civil disobedience with religious heresy.

The Shii clergy, however, were ambivalent and divided. They rejected the early dynasties, arguing that the Prophet's true heirs should have been the Twelve Imams. This line began with Ali, the Prophet's first cousin, son-in-law, and, according to the Shii clergy, designated successor, as the imam of the Muslim community. The line went through Ali's son Hosayn, the Third Imam, who rebelled against Yazid, the usurper caliph, and was martyred at the battle of Karbala forty-eight years after the Prophet's death. It ended with the last of their direct male descendants, the Twelfth Imam, also known as the Mahdi (Messiah), the Imam-e Montazar (Expected Leader), and the Sahab-e Zaman (Lord of the Age). He supposedly went into hiding a century after Hosayn's martyrdom but will appear at some future time when the world is rampant with corruption and oppression to prepare the way for Judgment Day.

Although the Shii clergy agreed that only the Hidden Imam had full legitimacy, they differed sharply among themselves regarding the existing states—even Shii ones. Some argued that since all rulers were in essence usurpers, true believers should shun the authorities like the plague. They should decline government positions; avoid Friday prayers, where thanks were invariably offered to the monarch; take disputes to their own legal experts rather than to the state judges; practice *taqiyya* (dissimulation) when in danger; and pay *khoms* (religious taxes), not to the government but to their clerical leaders, in their capacity as Nayeb-e Imam (Imam's Deputies).

Others, however, argued that one should grudgingly accept the state. They claimed that bad government was better than no government; that many imams had categorically opposed armed insurrections; and that Imam Ali, in his often quoted *Nahj al-Balaghah* (Way of eloquence), had warned of the dangers of social chaos. They also pointed out that Jafar Sadeq, the sixth and most scholarly of the imams, had stressed: "If your ruler is bad, ask God to reform him; but if he is good, ask God to prolong his life."

Others wholeheartedly accepted the state—especially after 1501, when the Safavids established a Shii dynasty in Iran. Following the example of Majlisi, the well-known Safavid theologian, they complied with the view that the shahs were "shadows of God on earth," obedience was the divine right of the shahs, political dissent led directly to damnation in the next world, without monarchy there would inevitably be social anarchy, and kings and clerics were complementary pillars of the state, sharing the imam's mantle. In making these arguments, these clerics often quoted not only al-Ghazzali but also the famous Koranic commandment "Obey those among you who have authority." In this form the Shii concept of the state was the mirror image of that of the conservative Sunnis.

It is significant that in all these discussions, which lasted on and off for some eleven centuries, no Shii writer ever explicitly contended that monarchies per se were illegitimate or that the senior clergy had the authority to control the state.[11] Most viewed the clergy's main responsibilities, which they referred to as the *velayat-e faqih* (jurist's guardianship), as being predominantly apolitical. They were to study the law based on the Koran, the Prophet's traditions, and the teachings of the Twelve Imams. They were also to use reason to update these laws; issue pronouncements on new problems; adjudicate in legal disputes; and distribute the *khoms* contributions to worthy widows, orphans, seminary students, and indigent male descendants of the Prophet. In fact, for most the term *velayat-e faqih* meant no more than the legal guardianship of the senior clerics over those deemed incapable of looking after their own interests—minors, widows, and the insane.

For a few, *velayat-e faqih* also meant that the senior clerics had the right to enter the political fray—but only temporarily and when the monarch clearly endangered the whole community. For example, in 1891 Mohammad Hasan Shirazi, one of the first clerics to be generally recognized as a *marja^c-e taqlid*, issued a decree against the government for selling a major tobacco concession to a British entrepreneur. He stressed, however, that he was merely opposed to bad court advisers and that he would withdraw from politics once the hated agreement was canceled. Similarly, in 1906, when the leading clerics participated in the Constitutional Revolution, their aim was neither to overthrow the monarchy nor to establish a theocracy but at most to set up a supervisory committee of senior clerics to ensure that legislation passed by the elected Parliament conformed to the sacred law.

Khomeini began his political career with typical Shii ambiguities. His first political tract, *Kashf al-Asrar* (1943), denounced the recently deposed Reza Shah for a host of secular sins: for closing down seminaries, expropriating religious endowments, propagating anticlerical sentiments, replacing religious courts with state ones, permitting the consumption of alcoholic beverages and the playing of "sensuous music," forcing men to wear Western-style hats, establishing coeducational schools, and banning the long veil *(chador)*, thereby "forcing women to go naked into the streets."[12] In this early work, however, he explicitly disavowed wanting to overthrow the throne and repeatedly reaffirmed his allegiance to monarchies in general and to "good monarchs" in particular. He argued that the Shii clergy had never opposed the state as such, even when governments had issued anti-Islamic orders, for "bad order was better than no order at all."[13] He emphasized that no cleric had ever claimed the right to rule; that many, including Majlisi, had supported their rulers, participated in government, and encouraged the faithful to pay taxes and cooperate with state authorities. If on rare occasions they had criticized their rulers, it was because they opposed specific monarchs, not the "whole foundation of monarchy." He also reminded his readers that Imam Ali had accepted "even the worst of the early caliphs."[14]

The most Khomeini asked in *Kashf al-Asrar* was that the monarch respect religion, recruit more clerics into Parliament *(maj-*

les), and ensure that state laws conformed with the sacred law. The sacred law, he argued, had prescriptions to remedy social ills; and the clergy, particularly the *fuqaha*, who specialized in the sacred law, were like highly trained doctors with knowledge of how to cure these social maladies.[15] Even though *Kashf al-Asrar* had limited demands, after the revolution Khomeini's disciples claimed his central ideas were all spelled out in this early tract.[16] However, one would search it in vain to find any discussion of such key subjects as revolution *(enqelab)*, republic *(jomhuri)*, martyrdom *(shahdat)*, the oppressed masses *(mostazafin)*, and even jurist's guardianship *(velayat-e faqih)*.

Khomeini retained traditional attitudes toward the state throughout the 1940s, 1950s, and 1960s. Even in 1963 when he emerged as the most vocal antiregime cleric, he did not call for a revolution or for the overthrow of the monarchy. Rather he castigated the shah for secular and antinational transgressions: becoming an unwitting tool of the "imperialist-Jewish conspiracy"; permitting women to vote in local elections; allowing citizens to take oaths on sacred books other than the Koran; smearing clerics as "black reactionaries"; trampling over the constitutional laws; giving high offices to the Bahais; siding with Israel against the Arabs, thus causing "our Sunni brothers to think that we Shiis are really Jews"; and "capitulating" to the almighty dollar by exempting American military personnel from Iranian laws. "An American cook," he declared, "can now assassinate our religious leaders or run over the shah without having to worry about our laws."[17]

These accusations were made more in the manner of a warning than of a revolutionary threat. Khomeini again reminded his audience that Imam Ali had accepted the caliphs.[18] He expressed "deep sorrow" that the shah continued to mistreat the clergy, whom he described as the "true guardians" of Islam.[19] He stressed that he wanted the young shah to reform so that he would not go the same way as his father, namely, into exile.[20] And even in 1965, after his own deportation, he continued to accept monarchies as legitimate. In one of his few proclamations issued in the mid-1960s, he exhorted Muslim monarchs to work together with Muslim republics against Israel.[21]

Khomeini did not develop a new concept of the state, or of

Figure 1. Stamp
(1981) honoring
Jalal al-Ahmad.

Figure 2. Stamp (1980)
honoring Ali Shariati.

society, until the late 1960s. It is not clear what intellectual influ-
ences brought about this change. Khomeini himself was reluctant
to admit formulating new notions. He was not in the habit of
footnoting his works and giving credit where credit was due—
especially if the sources were foreign or secular. What is more, in
the crucial years of 1965–70, when he was developing these new
ideas in his Najaf exile, he was conspicuously silent, rarely giving
interviews, sermons, and pronouncements.

We can therefore only speculate as to the origins of his new
ideas. One source may have been Shii theologians in Najaf, who
were forging new concepts while combating the Communist
party, which at the time had many adherents among Iraqi Shiis.[22]

They may have originated from Khomeini's younger Iranian students, more and more of whom were now coming from the lower middle class.[23] They may have been influenced by the famous ex-Tudeh writer Jalal al-Ahmad, whose pamphlet *Gharbzadegi* (The plague from the West) spearheaded the 1960s search for Islamic roots.[24] In fact, al-Ahmad was the only contemporary writer ever to obtain favorable comments from Khomeini. Even though al-Ahmad is famous for advocating a return to Islam, his works contained a strong Marxist flavor and analyzed society through a class perspective.

The views of other members of the Iranian intelligentsia, especially the Mojahedin, the Confederation of Iranian Students in Exile, and the radical pamphleteer Ali Shariati—all of whom were strongly influenced by contemporary Marxism, especially Castroism and Maoism—may have contributed to Khomeini's transition to political activist.[25] At one point, Khomeini inadvertently recognized the role played by the radical intelligentsia. In criticizing his apolitical colleagues, he declared that it was "disgraceful" that the clergy had remained "asleep" until "awakened" by protesting university students. "We cannot remain silent," he stressed, "until college students force us to carry out our duty."[26] One Khomeini disciple later admitted that the student guerrilla movement "left a deep impression on the Iranian people" and prompted the imam to increase his correspondence with the confederation in order to stem the influence of Marxism.[27]

It should also be noted that Khomeini formulated his new ideas at a time when social tensions within Iran were sharply increasing. Peasants were flooding the shantytowns in the cities. Small businessmen were feeling threatened by wealthy entrepreneurs linked to the central government and by the multinational corporations. "The American capitalists [*sarmayehdaran*]," declared Khomeini, "are scheming to take over Iran's natural resources."[28] Even more important, the Pahlavi state, bolstered by oil revenues, was slowly but surely encroaching upon the clerical establishment, especially its seminaries, publishing houses, and landed endowments. "The state," warned one opposition newspaper, "is out to nationalize religion."[29]

If what caused Khomeini to change his views is debatable, the actual changes are not. He broke his long silence in early 1970 with his famous lectures *Velayat-e Faqih: Hokumat-e Islami* (The jurist's guardianship: Islamic government). In these lectures, he declared in no uncertain terms that Islam was inherently incompatible with all forms of monarchy *(saltanat)*. He argued that monarchy was a "pagan" institution that the "despotic" Umayyads had adopted from the Roman and Sassanid empires. He also argued that the old prophets, particularly Moses, had opposed the pharaohs because they judged their royal titles to be immoral; and that Imam Hosayn had raised the banner of revolt in Karbala because he rejected hereditary kingship on principle. He further argued that monarchies were tantamount to false gods *(taqhut)*, idolatry *(shirk)*, and sowing corruption on earth *(fasid-e al-arz)*. The Prophet Mohammad had declared *malek al-muluk* (king of kings) to be the most hated of all titles in the eyes of the Almighty—Khomeini interpreted this title to be the equivalent of shah of shahs.

Muslims, Khomeini insisted, have the sacred duty to oppose all monarchies. They must not collaborate with them, have recourse to their institutions, pay for their bureaucracies, or practice dissimulation to protect themselves. On the contrary, they have the duty to rise up *(qiyam)* against them. Most kings, he added, have been criminals, oppressors, and mass murderers. In later years, he insisted that all monarchs without exception—including Shah Abbas, the famous Shii Safavid king, and Anushirvan, the ancient ruler whom Iranians usually refer to as "the Just"—had been thoroughly unjust.[30]

In denouncing kingship, Khomeini put forth various reasons why the religious judges *(fuqaha)* had the divine right to rule.[31] He sharply differentiated between the religious judges and other members of the senior clergy who specialized in other subjects, such as theology and history. He interpreted the Koranic commandment "Obey those among you who have authority" to mean that Muslims had to follow their religious judges. The Prophet had handed down to the imams all-encompassing authority—the right to lead and supervise the community as well as to interpret and implement the sacred law. The Twelfth

Imam, by going into hiding, had passed on this all-encompassing authority to the religious judges. Had not Imam Ali ordered "all believers to obey his successors"? Had he not explained that by "successors" he meant "those who transmit my statements and my traditions and teach them to the people"? Had not the Seventh Imam praised the religious judges as "the fortress of Islam"? Had not the Twelfth Imam instructed future generations to obey those who knew his teachings since they were his representatives among the people in the same way as he was God's representative among all believers? Had not the Prophet himself declared that knowledge led to paradise and that "men of knowledge" had as much superiority over ordinary mortals as the full moon had over the stars? Had not God created the sacred law to guide the community, the state to implement the sacred law, and the religious judges to understand and implement the sacred law? The religious judges, Khomeini concluded, have the "same authority" as the Prophet and the imams; and the term *velayat-e faqih* meant jurisdiction over believers, all of whom are in dire need of the sacred law. In other words, disobedience to the religious judges was disobedience to God.

In presenting his *Velayat-e Faqih*, Khomeini warned listeners that this "true Islam" might sound "strange."[32] After all, false ideas spread over the centuries by a conspiracy of Jews, imperialists, and royalists had taken a heavy toll. Important hadiths had been misinterpreted. The word *faqih* had been dropped out of important quotations. Government officials had systematically spread the notion that clerics should be seen within seminary confines and not heard in the arena of controversial politics, so much so that the crucial term *velayat-e faqih* had been distorted to refer only to the clergy's guardianship over widows, orphans, and the mentally incompetent. Despite these obstacles, Khomeini reminded his audience, clerics had risen to the occasion in times of crisis to protect Islam and Iran from imperialism and royal despotism: in the Tobacco Crisis of 1891, in the Constitutional Revolution of 1906, in the dark days of Reza Shah, and, of course, in the 1963 June Uprising against Mohammad Reza Shah. In these crises, Khomeini stressed, the clergy as a whole had kept alive "national consciousness" and stood firm as the "fortress of inde-

pendence'' against imperialism, secularism, and other "isms" imported from the West.[33]

Khomeini's View of Society

Khomeini's ideas about society developed along parallel lines with
his ideas about the state. In his pre-1970 writings, he tended to
accept the traditional notions of society as sketched out in Imam
Ali's *Nahj al-Balaghah,* in the teachings of the Shii clergy, and in
the "Mirror of Princes" literature produced throughout the centuries. He accepted the conventional paternalistic assumptions
that God had created both private property and society; society
should be formed of a hierarchy of mutually dependent strata
(qeshreha); the poor should accept their lot and not envy the rich;
and the rich should thank God, avoid conspicuous consumption,
and give generously to the poor. He often stressed that the sacred
law protected wealth as a "divine gift" and that the state had the
sacred duty to maintain a healthy balance between the social
strata.

It is significant that in these early writings he rarely used the
word *tabaqeh* (class)—a term that at the time had strong leftist
connotations. He also tended to avoid the word *enqelab* (revolution) even though he did occasionally call for a *qiyam* (uprising).
For the conventional clergy, *enqelab* connoted chaos, anarchy,
and class hatred. It was synonymous with the world turned upside
down.[34]

In his post-1970 writings, however, Khomeini depicted society
as sharply divided into two warring classes *(tabaqat):* the *mostazafin* (oppressed) against the *mostakberin* (oppressors); the
foqara (poor) against the *sarvatmandan* (rich); the *mellat-e mostazaf* (oppressed nation) against the *hokumat-e shaytan* (Satan's
government); the *zagheh-neshinha* (slum dwellers) against the
kakh-neshinha (palace dwellers); the *tabaqeh-e payin* (lower
class) against the *tabaqeh-e bala* (upper class); and *tabaqeh-e
mostamdan* (needy class) against the *tabaqeh-e a^{c}yan* (aristocratic class). In the past, such imagery would have been used by

secular leftists rather than by clerical leaders. The fact that Khomeini—the country's most successful politician—came to power by openly exploiting class antagonisms should undermine the notion favored by many Western social scientists that class analysis is not applicable to Iran.

The key to Khomeini's transformation can be seen in the way he used the words *mostazafin* and *shahid* (martyr). He rarely used the former in his early writings. When he did, it was in the Koranic sense of the "humble" and passive "meek" believers, especially orphans, widows, and the mentally impaired. In the 1970s, however, he used it in almost every single speech and proclamation to depict the angry poor, the "exploited" people, and the "downtrodden masses." After the revolution, he gradually broadened the term to bring in the propertied middle class, which actively supported the new order. Thus by mid-1980, *mostazafin* was a broad subjective category bearing striking resemblance to the Jacobin *sans culottes*, Sukarno's *Manrhaen* commonfolk, Perón's *descamisados* (coatless ones), and Vargas's *trabalhadores* (urban workers).

Shahid also went through a similar transformation. In his early works, Khomeini rarely used the term, and when he did, it was usually in the conventional sense of the famous Shii saints who, in obeying God's will, had gone to their deaths. He rarely used it to refer to the average person in the street who had died for the cause. For example, in his 1963–64 proclamations he described those killed in the June Uprising not as *shahidha* but as *bicharehha* (unfortunate ones). During the revolution, however, Khomeini constantly lauded anyone killed in the streets as a glorious *shahid*—as a revolutionary martyr.

In this, as in much of his other rhetoric, Khomeini was following in the footsteps of others. In 1964, the Tudeh party had published a roll book of Communists killed by the Pahlavis, *Yadnameh-e Shahidan* (Martyrs' memorial).[35] In the late 1960s, the Mojahedin had written a famous pamphlet, *Nahzat-e Hosayni* (Hosayn's movement), arguing that the early Shii martyrs had taken up arms to overthrow an exploitative regime, like Che Guevara, and had set an example for other revolutionaries

Figure 3.   Poster urging the construction of housing for the poor. Courtesy of the Hoover Institution.

Figure 4. Poster of peasants reading a newspaper. Courtesy of the Hoover Institution.

throughout the world.[36] In the early 1970s, Shariati had given a number of lectures on martyrdom in which he had insisted that true believers had a sacred duty to struggle, and if necessary to make the supreme sacrifice, in order to liberate their country from class oppression and colonial domination.[37] Shariati popularized a nineteenth-century saying, "Every place should be turned into Karbala, every month into Moharram, and every day into Ashura." Khomeini later adopted this as one of his own slogans.[38]

Similarly in the early 1970s, Hojjat al-Islam Nimatollah Salahi-Najafabadi had published in Qom a highly controversial book entitled *Shahid-e Javid* (The eternal martyr). He argued that Imam Hosayn had taken up arms not because he sought dynastic power, as the Sunnis charged, nor because he was blindly following divine fate, as conventional Shiis claimed, but because he had calculated rationally that he had a good chance of overthrowing the oppressive regime.[39] Martyrdom, thus, was not just a saintly act but a revolutionary sacrifice to overthrow a despotic political order. This was probably the most controversial book written by a cleric in the decade before the revolution. Hojjat al-Islam Sham-sabadi, a conservative cleric in Isfahan, denounced from his pulpit both the author and Ayatollah Hosayn Ali Montazeri, who had written the introduction to the book. Montazeri's supporters responded by murdering Shamsabadi and his family.

It should also be noted that Khomeini's public pronouncements in the 1970s rarely mentioned doctrinal issues, especially his highly controversial concept of *velayat-e faqih*. Some of his lay allies later complained that this avoidance had been part of a devious clerical scheme to dupe the public.[40] Khomeini's disciples countered that it was the liberals and leftists who had conspired to suppress the book *Velayat-e Faqih*.[41] Whatever the reasons, some of Khomeini's lay advisers, such as Sadeq Qotbzadeh, were ignorant enough of the concept that they were completely bewildered when they heard it for the first time months after the revolution.[42]

While judiciously avoiding doctrinal matters, Khomeini targeted the shah on a host of highly sensitive socioeconomic issues. He accused him of widening the gap between rich and poor; favoring cronies, relatives, senior officials, and other *kravatis* (tie wearers); wasting oil resources on the ever-expanding army and bureaucracy; setting up assembly plants, not real manufacturing industries; ignoring the countryside in the distribution of essential services, including clinics, schools, electricity, and public baths; failing to give land to the landless peasantry; condemning the working class to a life of poverty, misery, and drudgery; creating huge shantytowns and neglecting low-income housing; bankrupting the bazaars by refusing to protect them from foreign competition and the superrich entrepreneurs; and compounding social problems by failing to combat rising crime, alcoholism, prostitution, and drug addiction.[43]

At the same time, Khomeini continued to denounce the shah for supporting the United States and Israel against the Arab world; trampling political liberties, especially the constitutional laws; making the country increasingly dependent on the West; and using cultural imperialism to undermine Islam and Iran. Islam was endangered, Khomeini constantly warned, from outside by imperialism and Zionism and from inside by such fifth columnists as monarchists, leftists, and other secularists.

These denunciations freely used highly radical, populist catchphrases, but careful scrutiny of Khomeini's rhetoric shows him to have been remarkably vague on specifics—especially on the question of private property. These catchphrases, including the following, were later adopted as demonstration slogans:[44]

Islam belongs to the oppressed, not to the oppressors.

Islam is for equality and social justice.

Islam represents the slum dwellers, not the palace dwellers.

Islam will eliminate class differences.

We are for Islam, not for capitalism and feudalism.

Islam originates from the masses, not from the rich.

In a truly Islamic society, there will be no shantytowns.

In a truly Islamic society, there will be no landless peasants.

The duty of the clergy is to liberate the hungry from the clutches of the rich.

Islam is not the opiate of the masses.

The poor were for the Prophet; the rich were against him.

The poor died for the Islamic Revolution; the rich plotted against it.

The martyrs of the Islamic Revolution were all members of lower classes: peasants, industrial workers, and bazaar merchants and tradesmen.

Oppressed of the world, unite.

The oppressed of the world should create a Party of the Oppressed.

The problems of the East come from the West—especially from American imperialism.

Neither West nor East, but Islam.

The oppressed nations of the world should unite against
   their imperialist oppressors.

Khomeini reinterpreted early Islamic history to reinforce
these populist notions. He argued that contrary to popular tradition, the Prophet had been a humble shepherd, not a successful
businessman; Imam Ali had been a penniless water carrier, not a
prosperous merchant; and many of the early prophets had been
simple laborers who had looked forward to the day when the
oppressed would become the oppressors, and the oppressors
would become the oppressed. He also argued that most of the
Shii clergy, including the grand ayatollahs, had originated from
the common people, lived like "humble folk," and died with few
worldly possessions.[45]

This populist rhetoric reached a crescendo in 1979. As the old
regime was collapsing, Khomeini incorporated into his political
vocabulary two words he had hitherto scrupulously avoided: *enqelab* and *jomhuri*. He now argued that the Islamic Revolution
would pave the way for an Islamic republic, which, in turn, would
hasten the establishment of a truly Islamic society. This society,
the exact opposite of Pahlavi Iran, would be free of want, hunger,
unemployment, slums, inequality, illiteracy, crime, alcoholism,
prostitution, drugs, nepotism, corruption, exploitation, foreign
domination, and, yes, even bureaucratic red tape. It would be a
society based on equality, fraternity, and social justice.

In promising utopia, Khomeini managed to discard two other
important tenets of traditional Shiism. For centuries, Shiis had
looked back longingly on Mohammad's Mecca and Imam Ali's
caliphate as the Golden Age of Islam. Khomeini now declared that
revolutionary Iran had already surpassed these early societies and
their insoluble problems. For centuries, Shiis had believed that the
Mahdi would return when the world was overflowing with injustice and tyranny. Khomeini now argued that the Mahdi would
reappear when Muslims had returned to Islam, created a just
society, and exported their revolution to other countries.[46] The
traditional quietist belief had been turned inside out.

The Constitution of the Islamic Republic and Khomeini's Political Testament

Khomeini's populism is revealed in the two most important texts published since the revolution: the Constitution of the Islamic Republic and Khomeini's *Matn-e Kamel-e Vasiyatnameh-e Elahi va Siyasi-ye Imam Khomeini* (The complete text of Imam Khomeini's divine will and political testament). The constitution was drafted in 1979–80 by an Assembly of Experts (Majles-e Khobregan)—most of whom were Khomeini's disciples. The political testament was drawn up in 1983, revised in the mid-1980s, and published immediately after Khomeini's death in June 1989.

The Constitution

At first glance, the text of the constitution with its 175 clauses reads like a cumbersome "fundamentalist" document.[47] It begins with the declaration that the Islamic Republic is based on the "principal faiths" of the justice of God; the existence of one God and submission to His will; the divine message and its fundamental role in all human laws; and the concept of the Resurrection and its "role in human evolution." It also declares that the leadership clauses, especially those stipulating that ultimate authority resides in the senior religious jurists, were to endure until the Mahdi, the Lord of the Age, reappeared on earth. This, however, did not prevent the Assembly of Experts from drastically revamping these clauses ten years later and even introducing a theological exam to keep more radical clerics out of this exclusive club.

A closer look, however, shows that the text of the constitution, not to mention its pretext, subtext, and context, is highly nonfundamentalist. Its central structure was taken straight from the French Fifth Republic, with Montesquieu's separation of powers. It divides the government into the executive, headed by the president, supervising a highly centralized state; the judiciary, with powers to appoint district judges and review their verdicts; and the national Parliament, elected through universal adult suffrage. For years Khomeini had argued that women's suffrage was un-

Islamic. He now argued that to deprive women of the vote was un-Islamic.

Superimposed on this conventional constitution was Khomeini's concept of *velayat-e faqih*. Khomeini, described as the Supreme Religious Jurist, was given the authority to dismiss the president, appoint the main military commanders, declare war and peace, and name senior clerics to the Guardian Council (Shawra-ye Negahban), whose chief responsibility was to ensure that all laws passed by Parliament conformed to the sacred law. The constitution added that if no supreme religious judge emerged after Khomeini, the leadership would pass to a committee of three or five senior clerics *(maraje^c-e taqlid)* to be chosen by the popularly elected Assembly of Experts. Najafabadi, the author of the controversial *Shahid-e Javid*, argued in a new book entitled *Velayat-e Faqih: Hokumat-e Salihan* (Jurist's guardianship: Worthy government) that this two-stage electoral process would help harmonize the concepts of divine rule and clerical supervision with those of popular sovereignty and majority representation.[48] He also argued that the concept of *velayat-e faqih* implicitly involved the notion of a "social contract" between the religious judges and the population.

Although Khomeini's death left the country with no obvious successor, the clause stipulating that a committee of senior clerics should take his place was never enacted. Rather, the Assembly of Experts, knowing well that the senior jurists distrusted their version of Islam, quickly amended the constitution. They dropped the *marja^c-e taqlid* requirement so that Khomeini's position could be inherited by Hojjat al-Islam Ali Khamenei—a middle-ranking cleric who was neither a senior religious jurist nor a *marja^c-e taqlid*, nor at the time even a generally accepted ayatollah. This amendment, while revealing the pragmatic nature of Khomeinism, unwittingly undermined the intellectual foundations of Khomeini's *velayat-e faqih*. After all, in his *Velayat-e Faqih* Khomeini had argued that only the most senior religious jurists—not just any cleric—had the scholastic expertise and the educational training to fully comprehend the intricacies of Islamic jurisprudence.

In fact, Khomeini himself, anticipating the succession problem, had begun to modify his *velayat-e faqih* concept at the very end of his life. In March 1989, three months before his death, he made a major pronouncement categorizing the clergy into two distinct groups: those most knowledgeable about religious scholarship, including the sacred law, and those most knowledgeable about the contemporary world, especially economic, social, and political matters.[49] The latter, he declared, should rule because they were more in touch with the "problems of the day." After two decades of insisting that the religious jurists should rule, he was now arguing that the political clergy should be the ultimate authority. After a lifetime of denouncing secularism as a Western perversion, he was now close to concluding that the affairs of this world were separate from the understanding of the sacred law. The shift reflected the mind of a political pragmatist, not a religious fundamentalist.

The Constitution of the Islamic Republic contained much populist rhetoric. It began with the two controversial terms *enqelab* and *jomhuri*. It glorified Khomeini not only as the revolution's leader *(rahbar)*, the republic's founder, and the most respected of the religious jurists, but also as an imam, a title Iranian Shiis had traditionally reserved for the revered original Twelve Imams. In fact, some conservative clerics viewed this novel use of the title imam as somewhat blasphemous.[50]

The constitution went on to promise all citizens pensions, social security, unemployment benefits, disability pay, medical services, and free secondary as well as primary school education. It promised to eradicate hoarding, usury, monopolies, unemployment, poverty, and social deprivation; provide interest-free loans; utilize science and technology; and "plan the economy in such a way that all individuals will have the time and opportunity to enhance their moral and social development and participate in the leadership and management of the country." These clauses seem to have escaped the notice of Western journalists who claim that the

Iranian revolution was carried out in the name of rejecting this
type of society. In fact, the Iranian constitution has far more to say
about economic matters than most Western constitutions. It
promises to make Iran fully independent, pay off external loans,
cancel foreign concessions, nationalize foreign companies, strive
for the total unity of all Muslims, and "help the oppressed of the
world struggle against their oppressors."

Despite the radical rhetoric, the constitution undertook to safe-
guard private property. It pledged to balance the government
budget, encourage "home ownership," and respect the predomi-
nance of the "private sector" in agriculture, trade, services, and
small industries. What is more, it intentionally avoided the term
nezam-e tawhidi (monotheistic order), a term that the Mojahedin
wanted enshrined in the constitution as the republic's ultimate
goal. These full-fledged radicals, as opposed to mere populists,
had championed the term and given it connotations similar to the
Marxist notion of the "classless society."

Khomeini's Divine Will and Political Testament

Khomeini's thirty-five-page handwritten will is coherently struc-
tured, even though it went through major alterations between its
composition and its eventual publication.[51] Its prologue hails true
Islam as the message of "liberation" and "social justice" not just
for Iranians and Muslims but also for the "oppressed people of the
world irrespective of nationality and religion." It also claims that
the true message of Islam is being constantly distorted by an
international conspiracy of Zionists, Communists, Eastern and
Western imperialists, Marxists masquerading as Muslims, West-
ern-contaminated liberals, opportunistic clerics, and local tyrants
(namely, the Saudis in Arabia, King Hasan of Morocco, King
Hosayn of Jordan, and Saddam Hosayn of Iraq).

The text has sections addressed to specific groups: the clergy
and the seminaries; the university-educated intelligentsia; the parliamentary deputies; the judiciary; the executive, particularly the
cabinet; the armed forces, including the regular army as well as
the Revolutionary Guards; the mass media, including the radio-

television network and the daily newspapers; the opposition in exile, especially the Marxist parties; and, last but not least, the bazaars with their shopkeepers, traders, and small businessmen. In each section, he warns of the ever present danger of conspiracies hatched by the superpowers and fifth columnists.

In addressing Parliament, Khomeini stresses that the deputies should continue to come from the "middle class and the deprived population" and not from the ranks of the "capitalists, land-grabbers, and the upper class, who lust in pleasure and know nothing about hunger, poverty, and barefootedness." He reminds the ministers and civil servants that the revolution succeeded because of the active participation of the "deprived classes." He warns that if they lose this support they will follow the Pahlavis into exile.

In addressing the bazaars, he emphasizes that Islam safeguards private property. It encourages private investments in agriculture and industry, provides for a "balanced economy in which the private sector is recognized," and, unlike communism, respects private property for providing "social justice" and turning the "wheels of a healthy economy." He ends his last testament by telling Muslims and the deprived of the world that they should not sit around passively waiting for liberation but should rise up to overthrow the imperialists and their local lackeys—the tyrants, the palace dwellers, and those indulging in conspicuous consumption.

Khomeinism and Populism

Khomeinism, despite its religious dimension, in many ways resembles Latin American populism. This is not surprising, because Pahlavi Iran had much in common with Latin America: an informal rather than formal dependence on the West; an upper class that included a comprador bourgeoisie; an anti-imperialist middle class; an urban working class unorganized by the Left; and a recent influx of rural migrants into urban shantytowns.

Khomeinism, like Latin American populism, was mainly a

middle-class movement that mobilized the masses with radical-sounding rhetoric against the external powers and the entrenched power-holding classes, including the comprador bourgeoisie. In attacking the establishment, however, it was careful to respect private property and avoid concrete proposals that would undermine the petty bourgeoisie. These movements had vague aspirations and no precise programs. Their rhetoric was more important than their programs and blueprints. They used the language of class against the ruling elite, but once the old order was swept aside, they stressed the need for communal solidarity and national unity. They turned out to be more interested in changing cultural and educational institutions than in overthrowing the modes of production and distribution. They were Janus-faced: revolutionary against the old regimes and conservative once the new order was set up. The revolutionary aspect accounted for the initial endorsement from the Left. Religious fundamentalism could never have won this type of support.

Khomeinism, like Latin American populism, claimed to be a return to "native roots" and a means for eradicating "cosmopolitan ideas" and charting a noncapitalist, noncommunist "third way" toward development. In actual fact, however, many of the slogans and key concepts were borrowed from the outside world, especially from Europe. Khomeinism used organizations and plebiscitary politics to mobilize the masses, but at the same time it distrusted any form of political pluralism, liberalism, and grassroots democracy. Khomeinism developed ambiguous and contradictory attitudes toward the state. On the one hand, it wanted to protect middle-class property. On the other hand, it wanted to strengthen the state by extending its reach throughout society and providing social benefits to the lower classes. Khomeinism, strikingly like other populisms, elevated its leader into a demigod towering above the people and embodying their historical roots, future destiny, and revolutionary martyrs. Despite all the talk about the people, power emanated down from the leader, not up from the masses. Thus the title of imam should be seen not as purely religious but as the Shii-Iranian version of the Latin American El Lider, El Conductor, Jefe Maximo (Chief Boss), and O Paid do Povo (Father of the Poor).

2

Perceptions of Private Property,
Society, and the State

Wealth is a gift from God.
Ayatollah Khomeini, Ettela^cat,
29 December 1980

Introduction

Khomeini was no more a political philosopher than Molière's
bourgeois gentilhomme was a literary deconstructionist. He was,
first and foremost, a clerical leader who found himself immersed in
politics, and therefore felt compelled to express views on human
nature, social justice, class structure, legal authority, and state
power—in short, on political theory. Since his views were often
prompted by immediate and changing circumstances, it is not
surprising that they contain contradictions and inconsistencies—
so much so, that some scholars have described him as an archconservative, others as a fundamentalist reactionary, and others as a
"revolutionary radical," even as a "socialistic egalitarian."[1] The
intention of this chapter is neither to turn Khomeini into a political
philosopher nor to deny his conceptual inconsistencies. Rather, the
intention is to understand his political concepts by analyzing his
perceptions of private property, society, and the state.

Private Property

In his forty-six years of political activity, Khomeini shifted ground
on many issues, but he remained remarkably steadfast on the

39

crucial issue of private property. In his first major work, *Kashf al-Asrar*, he argued that Islam "protects private property" and by definition opposes dictators, who by their very nature threaten personal possessions.[2] Nevertheless, he argued, governments are necessary because human beings are naturally evil—greedy, egoistic, dangerous, and rapacious. Without government, there would be no law and order; without law and order, there would be no security for life and property. He also argued that God had endowed man with private property, and consequently, no one had the right to deprive another of this divine gift. He underlined this theme by reminding his readers that the sacred law categorically safeguarded private property, and since the sacred law was divinely inspired, it followed that no earthly power had the right to interfere with private property.

Kashf al-Asrar favored not only private property but also the propertied middle class. It urged the government to set up a special fund to help bankrupt businessmen.[3] It further urged the government to stop levying import-export duties on Iranian merchants on the grounds that such taxes were burdensome, unlawful, and against the interests of free trade.[4] It should be noted that Khomeini wrote *Kashf al-Asrar* at the request of a group of wealthy bazaaris who had opposed Reza Shah's policy of building a centralized secular state.[5]

In *Towzih al-Masa'el*, Khomeini continued the long Shii tradition of protecting private property in doctrinal issues. While discussing in what circumstances Muslims could be exhumed, he argued—as his predecessors had—that such a drastic act would be justified if the body was buried with someone else's belongings or in someone else's land without their permission.[6] In short, respect for property was more important than respect for the dead. In discussing the *hajj* (pilgrimage to Mecca), he advised—again like his predecessors—that the expensive venture should be undertaken only by those who had enough "land, business, and real estate" to afford the trip.[7]

In *Velayat-e Faqih*, Khomeini again stressed that the sacred law protected private property. He emphasized that the security of one's home was inviolable; that Islamic government, unlike dictatorships, could not confiscate personal belongings; and that the highest religious authorities could not take from the faithful one cent more than permitted by the sacred law. Not even Prophet Mohammad and Imam Ali had had the authority to trample over people's lives and property.[8] The *Velayat-e Faqih* was first presented as a series of lectures in the main bazaar mosque in Najaf. It should also be noted that Khomeini's main financial supporter in these years in Najaf was a wealthy Iranian merchant.[9]

Similar ideas can be found throughout his public statements. In 1963, in commemorating a student massacre in Qom, he argued that since Islam gives full protection to people's property and homes, Muslims had the right to take up arms and, if necessary, to kill to defend their homes.[10] In 1964, in his famous anti-Capitulations proclamation that prompted his deportation, he accused the shah of handing the country's bazaars over to America and Israel.[11] In 1967, in his Moharram message, he argued that the so-called White Revolution was bankrupting the bazaars and the reputable merchants.[12] In 1971, during the celebrations for 2,500 years of monarchy, he protested that the shah was extracting huge sums from respectable bazaaris to pay for his extravaganzas.[13]

In 1978, while in Paris living in the house of a wealthy businessman, he told European journalists that the shah wanted to destroy the merchants because Iranians as a whole had high regard for their bazaars.[14] In 1979, during the collapse of the old order, he reminded the country, especially the Revolutionary Guards, that they could not violate the sanctity of citizens' homes and land.[15] He also argued on a number of occasions that Islam, unlike communism, recognized private property; that his followers had no intention of confiscating factories and farms;[16] that the Islamic Revolution, unlike others, would not endanger people's possessions;[17] and that the new order, in sharp contrast to the old one, would fully respect the privacy of people's homes.[18]

In 1980, in the midst of the revolutionary turmoil, Khomeini again stressed that "wealth is a gift from God."[19] He emphasized that the new republic, unlike the Qajar and Pahlavi monarchies, would not treat the country as a "feudal fiefdom";[20] and that no one, not even the clergy, had the right to violate people's farms, houses, and orchards.[21] In 1981, he frequently reminded the public that the shah had been determined to destroy small businessmen[22] and that without national independence there would be no real protection of private property.[23] In the same year, he issued with much publicity his famous Eight-Point Declaration, which ordered the revolutionary authorities to fully respect people's "movable and immovable possessions," including their homes, stores, workshops, farms, and factories.[24] They were even told not to tap the telephones of or otherwise spy on private homes.

Of course, it is true that revolutionary tribunals in this period often expropriated wealth, especially agribusinesses, large factories, and luxury homes belonging to the former elite. But it is also true that in expropriating this wealth, the tribunals carefully avoided challenging the concept of private property. Instead they accused their victims of political misdeeds, especially conspiring against the revolution. They were attacking not wealth per se, but wealthy individuals suspected of "counterrevolutionary crimes." In this regard, the Islamic Revolution behaved in much the same way as the English, French, and American revolutions. Few would describe these Western revolutions as threats against the bourgeois concept of private property.

Khomeini reiterated his commitment to private property in the last years of his life. He warned that judges who did not respect Muslim lives, property, and honor would be punished in this as well as the next world;[25] if the Iraqis won the war, they would plunder people's possessions;[26] if the Eight-Point Declaration was ignored, citizens' homes and privacy would be endangered;[27] and if the new regime violated "private property" as the previous one had done, it would meet the same fate.[28] Finally in his *Vasiyat-nameh-e Elahi va Siyasi*, he reminded the government that Islam "recognizes private property," free enterprise would turn the "wheels of the economy," and this, in turn, would produce "social justice" for all, especially the poor. "Islam," he proclaimed, "differs sharply from communism. Whereas the former respects private property, the latter advocates the sharing of all things—including wives and homosexuals."[29]

Ayatollah Mohammad Beheshti, the chief architect of the Constitution of the Islamic Republic, reflected Khomeini's views in many ways. In a series of articles entitled "Islam and Private Property," Beheshti argued that the Koran and the Shii traditions protect legitimate wealth (as opposed to illegitimate wealth, obtained by robbery, extortion, and prostitution) for the simple reason that human labor was the source of all such property.[30] This labor, he explained, was physical work, mental work, such as accountancy, or public service *(khedmat)*, especially trade and commerce. Some citizens became wealthier than others as a result of their hard work, their talent, or inheritance. Economic inequalities, especially in wages and salaries, could also be increased by legitimate market forces. Individuals, not society, owned property. The state, however, as the guardian of the community, was entitled to supervise "common property," namely, irrigation water, natural resources, and wastelands. The state could also intervene in the marketplace if the forces of supply and demand created "extreme" inequality in wages and salaries.

Similar arguments can be found in the works of Ayatollah Morteza Motahhari, a leading member of the Islamic Revolution, who, upon his assassination in 1979, was praised by Khomeini as "my son," "the product of my life," and "the outstanding thinker, philosopher, and senior jurist of Islamology."[31] According to Motahhari, God created private property, and therefore, the state has the divine duty to scrupulously respect it.[32] The state, of course, could collect legitimate taxes, dispose of wastelands, expropriate stolen goods, administer communal property, mine natural resources under the soil, regulate the sacred law's directives on inheritance, and, under exceptional circumstances, intervene in the marketplace to help the needy. Khomeinists hailed this as Islamic economics; skeptics could well describe it as conventional bourgeois economics tempered with a dose of welfare paternalism. This heavy emphasis placed on property rights undermines the claim made both by some Khomeinists and by Orientalists that Islam inherently advocates socioeconomic egalitarianism.

Although the Khomeinists resemble the Western bourgeoisie in their respect for private property, the two differ in their premises.

The latter, especially the Enlightenment philosophes, base their arguments on the theory of natural law, insisting that man is born with the inalienable right to liberty and property. The former, while sanctifying wealth as a "divine gift," tend to dismiss natural law as an alien and secular notion. The latter view mankind as naturally rational, even good, and, therefore, capable of respecting the rights of others. The former see the average human being as basically sinful—corrupt, greedy, irrational, and, in Khomeini's own words, "even more dangerous than the wildest jungle animals."[33] In this respect, Khomeini resembled Saint Augustine, Edmund Burke, and Joseph de Maistre, an early proponent of fascism, more than he did the Enlightenment philosophes.

These premises help explain why so many members of the Iranian bourgeoisie leaned toward authoritarian conclusions—conclusions that did not become self-evident until well after the Islamic Revolution.[34] The concept of natural law had liberated the Western bourgeoisie from the shackles of royal absolutism. The rejection of natural law meant that the Iranian bourgeoisie had no choice but to protect their possessions by appealing to the divine law and, thereby, linking property rights to the existence of a clerical state. The problem was compounded further by the fact that those who rejected natural law could not resort to the dominant traditional institutions to defend property rights—as Burke and others in Europe had done. After all, the monarchical institutions in Iran were reputed to have been gross violators of private property.

Thus, if property was a divine gift, as Khomeini argued, then the government, as long as it was God's government, had the ultimate right to defend and oversee private property. If mankind was inherently evil, irrational, and violent, then individual liberty was an open invitation to social chaos. Democracy paved the way to anarchy. Unbridled pluralism invited internal disorder. If individuals were instinctively rapacious, then strong authority was needed to preserve private property.[35] Without authority, social groups, as well as individuals, would violate the rights of others. Without guidance, the average person would be led astray by bestial passions; the average person, like orphans, widows, and the mentally incompetent, needed constant supervision.

Without the ever-present fear of the state, especially of the executioner, citizens would be tempted to violate their neighbors' rights and possessions. In light of this jaundiced view of human nature, one can view the imposition of public whippings and amputations not so much as the reintroduction of the medieval "discourse" on crime and punishment (in the Foucaultian sense) as the introduction of a modern, but fascistic, concept of political power: the essence of the state is the public executioner.[36] It should be noted, however, that some mavericks, such as Najafabadi, the controversial author of *Shahid-e Javid* and *Hokumat-e Salihan*, have tried to reconcile Shiism with the concepts of natural law, reason, and social contract.[37] Time will tell how far this line of argument can go.

Society

Although Khomeini's respect for private property remained unswerving, his notion of the optimal social structure passed through three distinct stages. In the first, which lasted from the 1940s until the late 1960s, his ideas were remarkably conventional and conservative. In the second, which continued through the revolutionary 1970s into the early 1980s, he adopted militant rhetoric, developing in the process his new version of Shii populism. In the last stage, from the consolidation of the new regime until his death, he gradually discarded the more radical rhetoric and articulated a less militant version of Shii populism.

The First Stage (1943–70): A Multilayered Hierarchy

At first Khomeini saw society as a multilayered hierarchy formed of many occupational groups *(qeshrha):* clerics and seminary students, landlords and tribal chiefs, civil servants and office employees, intellectuals and professionals, bazaar merchants and tradesmen, laborers, and peasants and tribesmen. Each stratum was dependent on others for survival, each had its own functions to perform, and each needed to respect the rights of the others. Khomeini's scheme was, to borrow Stanislaw Ossowski's terminology, that of "harmonious gradation."[38]

The government's main tasks were to protect Islam and maintain the proper balance between the strata. The clergy—whom Khomeini often defined as the "highest stratum" *(qeshr-e bala)*— had the responsibility of speaking out if the government did not carry out its main tasks. In fact, Khomeini in this period often used the Aristotelian metaphor of the "human body" to describe society. The various strata were each part of an organic whole and were by definition unequal. They were divinely ordained to respect and not to challenge their superiors—revolution was synonymous with anarchy, banditry, and bloodshed.[39] It is significant that in this period Khomeini implicitly accepted sharecropping and even slavery as legitimate and explicitly described certain low-status occupations, such as selling shrouds, as "loathsome."[40]

Even more "loathsome" were non-Muslims, including the traditionally tolerated "People of the Book"—the Jews, Christians, and Zoroastrians. Being non-Muslims, they were considered to be *kafer* (infidels) and thus, according to Shii Iranian tradition, were *najes* (unclean). Being unclean, they could not marry Muslims, touch the Koran, bury their dead in Muslim cemeteries, or use public places such as barbershops, town baths, and the streets during rainstorms, because their washed-away sweat could come in contact with Muslims. In fact, this Iranian use of the term *najes* has more in common with the Hindu notion of "untouchables" than with the Sunni concept of "contamination." The Sunnis, as well as the Shiis outside Iran, rule that believers have to be physically "uncontaminated" only when performing religious duties.

"The following eleven," in Khomeini's own words, "are *najes*. First, urine; second, stool; third, semen; fourth, dead bodies; fifth, blood; sixth and seventh, dogs and pigs; eighth, non-Muslims; ninth, wine; tenth, beer; eleventh, the sweat of a camel that eats unclean things."[41] Khomeini's main hagiographer boasts that the imam would not eat or drink in restaurants unless he knew for sure that the waiter was a Muslim.[42] It should be noted that however "unclean" the non-Muslims were, their property was to

be respected as long as they paid their special taxes, gave allegiance to the Muslim state, and functioned as separate, but unequal, communities. In this, as well as in his general attitude
toward religious minorities, Khomeini followed conventional Shii
Iranian traditions.

The Second Stage (1970–82): The Oppressors and the Oppressed

In this period Khomeini freely borrowed concepts, language, and
imagery from full-fledged radicals, especially the Mojahedin and
Ali Shariati. He now depicted society as formed of two antagonistic classes *(tabaqat):* the oppressed *(mostazafin)* and the oppressors *(mostakberin).* In the past, Khomeini had rarely used the
term *mostazafin,* and when he had, it had been in the Koranic
sense of "the meek," "the humble," and "the weak." He now
used it to mean the angry "oppressed masses," a meaning it had
acquired in the early 1960s when Shariati and his disciples translated Franz Fanon's *The Wretched of the Earth* as *Mostazafin-e
Zamin.*

By the eve of the revolution, Khomeini was portraying society
as divided into two warring classes, each with economic attri-
butes.[43] On one side was the upper class *(tabaqeh-e bala),* which
he identified, in his own terminology, as formed of the oppressors,
the rich, the exploiters, the powerful, the feudalists, the capitalists, the palace dwellers, the corrupt, the high and mighty, the
opulent, the enjoyers of luxury, the gluttonous, the lazy time-
servers, and the wealthy elite. On the other side was the lower
class *(tabaqeh-e payin):* the oppressed, the exploited, the power-
less, the slum dwellers, the barefooted, the street folk, the hardworking poor, the hungry, the unemployed, the disinherited
masses, and those deprived of education, work, housing, and
medical facilities.

The oppressors, Khomeini argued, had always favored unjust,
satanic, and tyrannical government. They had opposed the
Prophet Mohammad, subverted his message, and now supported
the Pahlavi monarchy and the imperialist Americans. The op-

pressed, on the other hand, had always struggled for a just and Islamic government. They had rallied behind the Prophet, remained true to his creed, and now were willing to die for the Islamic Revolution. Khomeini added that the clergy would lead the oppressed masses to their liberation.[44] He also implied that the lower class respected private property, whereas the upper class had no regard for other people's belongings.[45] In Ossowski's terminology, Khomeini's picture of society was now one of "antagonistic dichotomy."[46]

In this stage, Khomeini and his disciples often placed the religious minorities, especially the Jews and the Bahais, on the side of the oppressors. They referred to them as "traitors," "Zionists," "economic plunderers," and the "enemies of Islam, the clergy, and Muslim intellectuals."[47] However, they made no attempt to transform their concept of *najes* into actual discriminatory laws. Their distrust was expressed more in political than in religious-theological terms.

In formulating a dichotomous scheme of society, Khomeini frequently resorted to history. He asserted that Mohammad and Moses had been poor shepherds; Imam Ali had been a water carrier willing to give up his extra shirt to a needy believer; and Imam Ali, as caliph, had not used candles at night to help the public treasury. He argued that the Prophet's war with pagan Mecca had been a "class struggle" against the exploiters and that Imam Hosayn had died at Karbala trying to liberate the "oppressed from the clutches of the satanic despots." He also asserted that Islam had always found its true strength among the dispossessed masses; the martyrs of righteous protests, like the 1963 June Uprising, had all come from the lower class; and the senior clergy lived frugal lives and originated from the humble masses. Muslim leaders, he insisted, avoided family favoritism and treated relatives as they did other members of the community.

During the revolutionary 1970s Khomeini not only depicted society as class struggle but also promised to redistribute among the deprived masses the ill-gotten wealth of the foreign companies, the Pahlavi family, and the rich courtiers.[48] He also promised to establish on earth an Islamic utopia free of injustice, inequality, poverty, social conflict, unemployment, landlessness, foreign dependence, imperial exploitation, political oppression, social alienation, prostitution, alcoholism, drug addiction, crime, nepotism, government corruption, and bureaucratic red tape. "The Islamic Revolution," he declared, "will do more than liberate us from oppression and imperialism. It will create a new type of human being."[49] To hasten the arrival of this utopia he urged his followers to "unite the oppressed of the world, both Muslim and non-Muslim, against their class oppressors and foreign exploiters."[50]

Khomeini's disciples portrayed him as the ideal "man of the people." For example, a group of former students compiled a six-volume book of reminiscences dwelling mostly on his concern for others and disregard for his own material comforts.[51] They described him as living a humble life, "like an ordinary seminary student," eating simple food—bread, cheese, watermelons, and *abgusht* (the perennial poor man's stew)—wearing the same plain but clean clothes for years on end, and owning only two turbans, one for summer, the other for winter. They claimed that he took early morning walks in the street without bodyguards, even in France. When they searched for a house in Neauphle-le-Château outside Paris, he instructed them to find a "peasant" home. When they looked for a Tehran residence at the time of his triumphant return, he told them to avoid the northern, wealthy suburbs and search instead in the southern, *"mostazafin"* districts. In actual fact, they moved him temporarily to the Refah School, a private school funded by bazaari philanthropists and located in the lower-middle-class district of central Tehran.[52]

These disciples describe him as doing his own chores, not bothering his wife and servants, and even helping out in the kitchen when too many guests appeared. One writes that he made a special point of giving audiences to humble folk. Another writes that he was so determined to keep in touch with popular culture that he read from cover to cover a thousand-page bestseller entitled *Showhar-e Ahu Khanum* (The husband of Ahu Khanum). Written by a former Tudeh army officer who had been sentenced to life imprisonment, this popular novel focused on the problems of polygamy in a bazaari family.

He was praised for traits which others would recognize from the "Protestant ethic": frugality, modesty, punctuality, and impartiality. He refused to accept from bazaari admirers such luxuries as fancy carpets, air conditioners, private cars, and a summer vacation away from the Najaf heat. When friends tried to replace his broken-down furniture, he retorted, "This is not the home of a government minister." When they tried to repaint his house, he replied that peeling walls did not bother him.

He scolded others for leaving lights on, throwing away drinking water, and wasting money on taxis. At Neauphle-le-Château, he ordered his household to return the many oranges they had purchased on sale with the argument they did not need so many and such a large transaction would drive up the prices and thus would be unfair to the local population. He denied himself personal long-distance phone calls, even when his son Mostafa died. He disliked favoritism, treating his sons as he did the rest of his many students. He kept meticulous financial records and scrupulously separated personal expenses from his office budget. He would not tolerate idle talk, especially backbiting gossip. He canceled classes for three days when he overheard a student making rude remarks about another *marja^c-e taqlid*. He was so punctual and his schedule was so routine that members of his household claimed they could set their watches by his daily activities.

When Borujerdi died Khomeini went into seclusion so that his students would not publicly acclaim him as a new *marja^c-e taqlid*. They had to plead with him to get him to publish his *Towzih al-Masa'el* so that he would be recognized by others as a grand ayatollah. They quoted him as saying that he preferred to remain a "humble teacher and scholar." They claim that when Ayatollah Hakim, another senior cleric, died in 1968, Khomeini again ordered his followers not to campaign on his behalf for the title of supreme *marja^c-e taqlid*. For his disciples, this modesty proved not only that Khomeini was a man of the people but also that he possessed the prerequisite quality needed to lead the Islamic community.

Figure 5. Stamp
(1982) honoring Jesus.
The inscription is in
Armenian and Arabic
as well as in Persian.

The Third Stage (1982–89): Recognition of the Middle Class

Khomeini's populist rhetoric proved to be highly explosive in postrevolutionary Iran, arousing anger not just against the royalist elite and the multinational corporations but also against the propertied middle class, particularly the religious minorities. Khomeini, therefore, began to tone down his language. He thanked the minorities, including the Jews, for producing "martyrs" in the struggle against the shah.[53] He distinguished Judaism, an "honorable religion that had arisen among the common folk," from Zionism, a "political 'ism' that opposed religion and supported the exploiters."[54] He argued that Imam Ali had treated all as equal and had not distinguished between Muslim and Jew.[55] As a gesture of goodwill toward the Christians, the Islamic Republic issued a postage stamp bearing Jesus' silhouette and a Koranic verse in Armenian—the first time Armenian had appeared on a stamp since the fall of the Armenian Republic in 1921. Khomeini also watered down his class rhetoric. He now argued that Islam wanted harmonious relationships between factory owners and workers, between landlords and peasants. "If these class antagonisms are not alleviated," he warned, "their inevitable explosion would destroy the whole Islamic Republic."[56]

In softening his rhetoric, Khomeini replaced his dichotomous image of society with a trichotomous one. He now increasingly delineated three main classes: an upper class *(tabaqeh-e bala)* formed of the remnants of the old wealthy families; a middle class *(tabaqeh-e motavasset)* composed of clerics, intellectuals, civil servants, merchants, shopkeepers, and tradesmen; and a lower class *(tabaqeh-e payin)* comprising laborers, peasants, and slum dwellers. In Ossowski's terminology, Khomeini, the prerevolutionary, used a scheme of harmonious gradation; Khomeini, the revolutionary, one of antagonistic dichotomy; and Khomeini, the postrevolutionary, one of semiharmonious trichotomy.

In the new picture, the word *mostazafin* ceased to be an economic category depicting the deprived masses. Instead it became—like the term *sans culottes* in the French Revolution—a political label for the new regime's supporters and included wealthy bazaar merchants. "The bazaars," Khomeini stated, "are a crucial part of the deprived masses. Those martyred in the revolution came from the bazaars and the middle class as well as from the shantytowns."[57] In one speech, Khomeini declared that in the years after the revolution the deprived classes, namely, "the intellectuals, the clergy, the peasants, the workers, and the bazaaris," had carried much of the country's burdens.[58] In another, he argued that the revolution had been accomplished by the masses, including the "bazaaris and the middling sort of people [*mardom-e motavasset*]."[59] In a speech commemorating the June Uprising, he stated that the martyrs of 1963, as well as those of 1978–79, had all come from the lower classes—from "the peasants and workers, from Muslim tradesmen and merchants."[60] Similarly in the 1984 parliamentary elections, he declared that the revolution would be undone if the republic lost the support of the bazaaris, who, he stressed, had played such a critical role in overthrowing the shah.[61]

Khomeini's disciples echoed his new use of the term *mostazafin*. For example, Rafsanjani, in a Friday sermon devoted to the term, began by assuring his audience that Islam was the "motor of history" that drove mankind toward its final destination, where the *mostazafin* would "inherit the world."[62] He then criticized fellow revolutionaries for grossly misusing the term in order to heap exaggerated praises on the weak, the poor, and the economically deprived. This, he argued, was a mistake because the Koran used the term *mostazafin* as a subjective *(fekri)* category to describe those fighting oppression. The Koran had not used it objectively to define the poor, many of whom often accepted and even collaborated with their oppressors. The Islamic Revolution, he concluded, proved that fighters against oppression could come from all walks of life and from diverse social strata.[63]

The new picture of society emerged most clearly in a major speech given by Khomeini to the Parliament on the third anniversary of the revolution. He warned that parliamentary deputies must come predominantly from the "middle class," they should not strive to become "upper class," and they should always help the "lower class." "The revolution will remain secure," Khomeini concluded, "so long as the Parliament and the government are manned by members of the middle class."[64]

Khomeini now placed heavy emphasis on the importance of harmony between the middle and lower classes.[65] The country as a whole was constantly referred to as a *mostazafin* nation *(mellat-e mostazafin)*. Clerics, intellectuals, bazaaris, workers, and peasants were described as having common interests against imperialism and the old upper class. The clergy was viewed as historically and socially close to the bazaaris. The new government leaders, in contrast to the former "ruling class," were seen as coming from the ranks of the bazaaris, the traders, and the seminary students.[66]

Khomeini underlined his support for the bazaars in a long address to the merchants of Tehran. He praised the bazaars for building mosques and seminaries, for serving throughout history as the staunch pillar of Islam, and for having lent their support to the clergy in such crucial crises as the 1891 Tobacco Crisis and the 1905 Constitutional Revolution.[67] "Previous rulers," he continued, "did not dare to set foot in the bazaars. But things are very different now for the government and the bazaar. The president and the bazaaris are all brothers born among the common people." Hojjat al-Islam Ali Khamenei, his immediate successor, continued this line of reasoning. In a lecture to university students,

Khamenei argued that Islam respected the bazaar, the Koran had favorable things to say about trade and commerce, and socialists, not Muslims, associated business with theft, corruption, and exploitation. "The bazaars," he declared, "helped the Islamic Revolution and continue to be staunch supporters of the Islamic Republic."[68]

The State

The class forces unleashed by the revolution prompted Khomeini not only to redraw his picture of society but also to pay greater attention to the role of the state—an entity that had hardly figured in his early works. The contemporary state, he had liked to argue, should be no more complex than the early caliphate, in which Imam Ali had been able to administer a vast region from the corner of a simple mosque. God's will could be carried out without a vast army of tax collectors, bureaucrats, and military officers. The state's main functions were simple: to implement the sacred law, provide law and order, allow local judges to make swift and final decisions, keep a healthy balance between the social strata, spend no more than it collected in the *khoms* taxes, and, most significant of all, restrain people's evil instincts, especially their instinct to steal.[69]

In these early works, the state had been mentioned in terms not of how limited or extensive it should be but rather who should supervise it. In *Kashf al-Asrar*, Khomeini had accepted monarchies on condition they sought the advice and consent of the senior clerics. In *Velayat-e Faqih*, he had argued that monarchies were incompatible with Islam and that the clerical jurists had the divine right to rule. But in both works he had pictured the true Islamic state as a very limited one, which probably helped increase Khomeini's popularity among the middle class.

The political realities of revolutionary Iran pressed Khomeini to pay greater attention to the state. To run the country's vast array of social services, the Islamic Republic had no choice but to extend the large ministries and their regional departments. To consolidate power, it found it necessary to put in place a system of local committees *(komitehs)* and Revolutionary Guards (Sepah-e Pasdaran). To fight the war with Iraq, it retained the existing armed forces, drastically expanded the Revolutionary Guards, and also created the Reconstruction Crusade (Jahad-e Sazandegi) and the volunteer force known as the Mobilization Army (Sepah-e Basij). To curb the arbitrary behavior of local judges, it kept the conventional and cumbersome appeals system, which Khomeini had denounced for forty years as un-Islamic and against the sacred law. To alleviate public discontent, it introduced food rationing and price controls and periodically launched campaigns against speculators, hoarders, and price-gougers. To administer the recently nationalized enterprises, mostly confiscated from multinational corporations, the royal family, and their close associates, the new regime had to dramatically expand the bureaucratic machinery. Prophet Mohammad and Imam Ali may have been able to run the community from a mosque corner; Khomeini had to preside over a state bureaucracy three times larger than that of Mohammad Reza Shah.

It was not only the increasing bureaucracy that forced Khomeini to pay greater attention to the state. The inherent contradiction between his populistic rhetoric and his respect for private property led eventually to a major constitutional impasse. Attacks on wealth resounded in the halls of Parliament, especially among the majority bloc, who referred to themselves as "progressives" *(motaraqi)* and to their opponents as "procapitalists" *(sarmayehdari)*. Respect for property, however, found a receptive audience in the Guardian Council, the body with the constitutional authority to ensure that all parliamentary bills conformed to the sacred law. Not surprisingly, from 1981 to 1987 the Guardian Council vetoed some one hundred reform bills as violations against the sanctity of private property. These bills included land reform, labor legislation, progressive income tax, control over urban real-estate transactions, nationalization of foreign trade, and confiscation of the property of émigrés who had not been found guilty of having obtained their wealth through unlawful means.

The impasse was compounded by Khomeini's reluctance to alienate supporters among either the bazaars or the laboring classes. On some days, he would praise the "slum dwellers" for their frugality and denounce the "palace dwellers" for their conspicuous consumption.[70] On other days, he would lecture the ministers on the virtues of limited government and the dangers of an "overbloated state." He advised the ministers to supervise rather than control the economy and to encourage entrepreneurs to do what they did best, such as importing goods and managing small factories.[71] He warned that bureaucrats could not possibly administer a nation of forty million, the people had the right to participate in economic activities, and the bazaaris should be treated as honorable partners rather than as untrustworthy outsiders.[72] He also warned that the government should do its utmost to keep the support of the bazaaris, for they had been Islam's main pillar of strength throughout Iranian history. "Their alienation," he argued, "had undermined the [1905] Constitutional Revolution"[73] and the cooling of their support now could very well lead to the collapse of the Islamic Republic.[74] "This is not a communist country," he exclaimed, "where the state can violate private property, taking away people's farms and factories. No, this is an Islamic country, where we recognize private property and keep government within bounds."[75]

Khomeini's conflicting signals hardened the deadlock between Parliament and the Guardian Council. To loosen the deadlock, Khomeini in late 1987 and early 1988 tried to nudge the council into accepting some of the milder reform bills, such as income tax and a watered-down labor law. In doing so, he issued what turned out to be a highly controversial decree on the authority of the state.[76] He criticized the diehard traditionalists for misunderstanding the role of government, especially in the regulation of prices and social services. Because the Prophet had had absolute (*motlaq*) authority, because this authority had been passed on to his political successors, and because the Islamic Republic was now his true successor, it followed that the present state in Iran should have absolute authority.

He also brought into his ruling the Sunni concept of public interest *(maslahah)*, a doctrine that permitted the state to violate citizens' rights for the common good and for Islam's long-term interests. In the past, the Shii clergy had been wary of this concept for obvious reasons. "The government in Islam," Khomeini elaborated, "is a primary rule having precedence over secondary rulings such as praying, fasting, and performing the *hajj*. The government can destroy a private house to build a public highway as long as it pays compensation. It can destroy a mosque if that building endangers the community. It can cancel religious contracts if these contracts undermine the common good." In short, the state, so long as it was a truly Islamic state, could overrule the highest-ranking clerics and their interpretation of the sacred law.

Liberal Muslims were shocked. They interpreted Khomeini's decree to be not only a direct attack on private property but also a license for establishing a Hobbesian Leviathan—perhaps even a totalitarian behemoth. This new ruling, argued Bazargan's Liberation Movement, contradicted not only Khomeini's previous promises but also the norms of the sacred law, the Koran, and the sacred traditions; in short, it violated Islam.[77] The bad caliphs had undermined the Muslim community by ruling despotically, stealing people's possessions, and thus instigating "incredible class wars." The Liberation Movement concluded that the new decree could do the same, especially because the bazaaris had enthusiastically supported the revolution on the understanding that the new order would respect the sacred law and private property.

These fears, however, turned out to be overly alarmist. Khomeini's purpose was not to undermine private property but to strengthen the Islamic Republic, which, in his eyes, was the guardian of Islam and thus in the long run the true defender of private property. In Khomeini's view, Islam was synonymous with the sacred law, and this law, by definition, sanctified private property. Even the Prophet and the imams, with their absolute power, had not had the right to tamper with private property.[78] It followed that the Islamic Republic, as the embodiment of Islam, the sacred law, and the imams' traditions, would protect the fundamental rights of private property. Furthermore, the original Sunni concept of public interest, as expounded by al-Ghazzali and other classical theorists, had given the state unrestricted powers only insofar as the rulers behaved within the "essential norms" of the sacred law—that is, respected religion, life, intellect, lineage, and private property.[79]

In his last years, Khomeini continued to appoint conservative jurists to the Guardian Council—often with the advice and consent of Grand Ayatollahs Golpayegani and Marashi-Najafi, the two highly traditional *maraje^C-e taqlid* who had joined the revolutionary bandwagon late in the day. He advised Parliament not to draft bills that would antagonize the Guardian Council and set up an arbitration committee to iron out differences between them, but he gave more than half of its seats to the conservative jurists. The committee was named the Council for Determining the Public Interest of the Islamic Order (Majma'-e Tashkhis-e Maslahat-e Nezam-e Islami). Khomeini also continued to criticize the traditional clergy on a host of issues, including their opposition to music, chess, and television. But, significantly, he never once criticized them on the vital issue of private property. On the contrary, he publicly praised archconservative ministers who had opposed a labor law on the grounds that the eight-hour day did not appear in the Koran and that Muslim factory owners did not need legislation to tell them how to treat their workers. Finally in his *Vasiyatnameh-e Elahi va Siyasi*, Khomeini advised all three branches of government to nourish a mixed economy, respect private property, and encourage businessmen to invest money in productive ventures and give alms to the poor to ensure their own welfare "in this as well as in the next world."[80]

Thus Khomeini's intentions were not so much to undermine the middle class as to strengthen the Islamic Republic, which, in his eyes, was the main defender of the long-term interests of Islam, the sacred law, and thereby private property. Although Khomeini has often been hailed as the champion of the deprived masses, his own words show him to be much more the spokesman of the propertied middle class. For this reason alone the Islamic

Revolution can be considered a bourgeois revolution. If this sounds strange to Western ears it is only because the traditional middle class in Iran protected property rights by appealing not to the language of natural rights and the Enlightenment but to that of Shii Islam—of the Koran, the sacred law, and the Twelve Imams.

3

May Day in the Islamic Republic

> It is not only today that should be considered
> Workers' Day. Every day should be honored as
> Workers' Day. For labor is the source of all
> things, . . . even of Heaven and Hell.
>
> *Ayatollah Khomeini*, Ettela^cat, *2 May 1979*

Introduction

May 1, 1979, was a major public festival in Iran. Waves of joyful demonstrators poured into the streets celebrating International Workers' Day as well as "the true spring of freedom after the 2,500-year-old monarchy." Since then the Islamic Republic has continued to observe, in one way or another, May Day.

Nothing could be more incongruous. May Day is an "invented tradition" of the nineteenth-century socialist movement in the West.[1] It conjures up images of the Haymarket tragedy; Chicago martyrs at the gallows reaffirming their faith in socialism, anarchism, and atheism; heavy machinery, proletarian caps, and smokestacks; and Marx's Second International, not to mention Lenin's Third International. It also evokes industrialism, militant trade unionism, and socialist internationalism breaking down all forms of parochialism, especially of religion, nationality, and gender.[2] The Islamic Republic, on the other hand, views itself as the authentic embodiment of pure Islam; is highly conscious of the political potency of rituals, images, symbols, and language; and claims to reject all Western concepts, especially those of human-

60

ism, socialism, feminism, and, the most insidious of all, Marxism.

The incongruity, however, has a clear-cut explanation. The Khomeini regime, in advocating an Iranian variant of Third World populism, wants to mobilize the urban working class, forestall any threat from the secular Left, and, at the same time, bring as much of that Left as possible under its own hegemony. Meanwhile, May Day, although originally an imported tradition, has become over the years an integral part of the leftist tradition in Iran and has been observed whenever possible since 1921. It is associated with labor struggles of the past—with demonstrations, work stoppages, general strikes, and violent confrontations. What is more, it is the moment of historical awareness which all the Left, whether Stalinist, Maoist, Castroist, Trotskyist, or Social Democratic, meticulously observe. In fact, a mark of being on the Left in Iran is to observe May Day—sometimes as a counterfestival to the official religious and nationalistic holidays.

Thus in 1979 the Islamic regime, to prove its radical credentials and appropriate the leftist tradition, celebrated May Day with much fanfare and revolutionary rhetoric. Since then the celebrations have continued, but with less and less fanfare, radical promises, and free participation. In fact, the way May Day has been observed can be used to gauge how far Khomeini's populism has been toned down as his regime has established itself and become economically more conservative. In other words, May Day is a revealing lens through which to observe the Thermidor of the Islamic Revolution. By the late 1980s May Day no longer produced street rallies and freewheeling mass meetings but highly controlled and carefully orchestrated indoor shows designed to drum up support for the regime.

May Day as a Political Gathering (1921–41)

Left-wing groups in Iran, especially the Printers' Union in Tehran, began to celebrate May Day in the early 1920s. These early celebrations, however, invariably took the form of indoor gatherings, often in secret. Most were organized by the newly founded Communist and Socialist parties jointly with their ally in Tehran, the Central Council of Federated Trade Unions (CCFTU).

At its height in the mid-1920s the CCFTU had over 8,000 members from about sixteen unions. They included teachers and municipal employees; skilled craftsmen, particularly printers, cobblers, tailors, carpenters, masons, pharmacists, telegraphers, and postal and telephone workers; and relatively unskilled wage earners, such as bath attendants, bakery assistants, bricklayers, and the weavers from Tehran's sole modern factory. Much of the recruiting was done in the teahouses and coffeehouses found throughout the bazaar and the poorer neighborhoods. The CCFTU's leadership comprised not only left-wing intellectuals but also a surprising number of craftsmen, especially printers, masons, and cobblers. The unions were interdenominational, with Muslims and Christians (mostly Armenians and Assyrians) in both their leadership and rank and file. The CCFTU also had affiliated unions in the provinces, particularly among fishery and dockworkers in Enzeli, carpet weavers and tailors in Mashad, and textile weavers in Isfahan. In the late 1920s they were joined by oil workers in Khuzestan.[3]

The early celebrations avoided street rallies for two major reasons. First, outside the oil region, the industrial proletariat was too small. In 1925 the whole country had fewer than twenty modern industrial plants; only five of them were large factories. Second, the government restricted such street demonstrations. In the early 1920s Colonel Reza Khan, the commander in chief of the armed forces, imposed martial law on most cities. By the late 1920s he had seized the throne and was ruling the country with an iron fist. And by 1931 he had enacted the Anticollectivist Law, which banned all activities smacking of socialism, communism, and trade unionism.

The first May Day meeting was organized in 1921 by the CCFTU in Tehran.[4] A modest-sized crowd gathered in the large Shah Mosque in central Tehran. The printers even closed down most of the publishing houses to honor the day. That evening a left-wing drama group put on a three-act comedy in the Grand Hotel located in the fashionable part of northern Tehran.

In preparation for the day, *Haqiqat* (The truth), the trade union organ, published a long editorial on the significance of May 1 (Ardibehesht 11 in the Iranian solar calendar).[5] This editorial became the model for later May Day articles. It began with a brief history of the festival, stressing that it was a modern holiday to mark, on the one hand, the end of the rule of "feudalists, clergy, and aristocrats" and, on the other hand, the beginning of working-class enslavement by industrial capitalists and their factory system, with its tendency to produce mass unemployment. It continued with a description of how in 1889, on the centenary of the French Revolution, the Second International, with the encouragement of Engels, had chosen May Day as the date to demonstrate working-class solidarity, demand the eight-hour workday, and honor the martyrs of Chicago in 1887 and the Paris Commune in 1871. The article went on to explain how May Day had served not only to celebrate class solidarity but also to strike fear in the hearts of the bourgeoisie and the authorities, demand the eight-hour day, and mark the dawn of a new age of human liberation. It ended with the proclamation that the young Iranian proletariat now joined the international proletariat in demanding work, liberty, equality, fundamental reforms, freedom of expression, elimination of class privileges, an end to foreign exploitation, the lifting of martial law, and the recognition of May Day as a public holiday.

Similar May Day celebrations occurred throughout the 1920s. For example, in 1924 printers in Tehran organized a one-day strike, and fishery workers in Enzeli attended an indoor rally near the town docks.[6] In 1928 a picture of Lenin was displayed in the First of May Club in Rasht, prompting a government crackdown.[7] This club had been organized by a group of Armenian intellectuals and Muslim trade unionists to bring together men and women for political lectures and theatrical shows. In 1918 they had, in fact, organized the first International Womens' Day in Iran.[8]

Also in 1928, on the Friday closest to May 1, small groups of Communist activists, totaling no more than 800, quietly made their way to a picnic in a rented garden outside Tehran. The program included music, lectures on the meaning of May Day, and recitation of an ode to workers written by Lahuti, a well-known revolutionary poet who had fled to the Soviet Union.[9] Their May Day Manifesto called for the overthrow of the shah, the landlords, the mullas, and the capitalists.[10] Red flags were draped on the garden trees. After the picnic, some of the participants gate-crashed a small May Day gathering at the Socialist party clubhouse in northern Tehran. This disruption drew the attention of the police and probably prompted the closure of the clubhouse. One of the gate-crashers admitted years later that looking back on this incident he was embarrassed by his "ultraleft" infantile behavior.[11]

The largest of these early May Day celebrations came in 1929. Radicals in Mashad, many of them teachers, tailors, and carpet weavers, met secretly on an isolated hill a few miles outside the city to listen to lectures and sing revolutionary songs.[12] In Abadan, refinery workers who had recently formed an underground union sparked off a general strike throughout the oil industry by demanding recognition of the union, a minimum wage, replacement of foreigners with Iranians, worker representation in the oil company's labor office, and the acceptance of May Day as a paid holiday.[13] The strike was broken four days later when the provincial authorities, under orders from Reza Shah, moved troops into the region and rounded up over forty-five labor organizers—five of whom were kept in prison until Reza Shah's abdication in 1941. The British government "thanked" and "congratulated" the shah for having dealt "so speedily" with the crisis.[14] Although this strike has received scant mention in history books, at the time it was serious enough to prompt the dispatch of a British battleship to Abadan.[15]

In the same year in Tehran, small groups of radicals, this time totaling 2,000, gathered outside the city early in the morning for another picnic, where they listened to poetry, an hour-long lecture, and a band, many of whose players were union members. The picnic lasted until midafternoon and was paid for by the trade unions. The departing crowd was large enough to arouse the interest of the police, which led to the arrest of about fifty participants, one of whom died in prison, probably as a result of mistreatment.[16]

The last of these early May Day gatherings came in 1931. In early spring of that year, the Communist party organized an underground union in the newly founded Vatan textile mill in Isfahan.[17] On May Day, this union met secretly in a garden outside the city and drafted a list of demands, including the eight-hour day, union recognition, Friday pay, and an end to corporal punishment in the factories. The union also wanted management to refer to laborers as *kargaran* (workers) rather than as *^{c}amaleh-ha* (hired hands).[18] The meeting displayed banners with the slogan "Workers of the World Unite!" When management refused to negotiate, the workers struck. The strike continued for two weeks until management made concessions and the government arrested over thirty labor organizers, one of whom soon died in prison, again probably as a result of mistreatment.[19]

In the wake of this strike, Reza Shah decreed his Anticollectivist Law, which threatened labor organizers and advocates of radical ideas with ten years' imprisonment. This law was used on a number of occasions in the 1930s, the most famous being in May 1937 when the police arrested fifty-three intellectuals and labor organizers, accusing them of publishing a May Day Manifesto to incite strikes in the Vatan mill, the railways, and Tehran University.[20] This group became famous as the "Fifty-three." Dr. Taqi Arani, their leader and a professor of physics at Tehran University, was charged with writing a May Day Manifesto, the main evidence presented to the court. Found guilty, Arani died in prison, probably as a result of being placed in a typhus-infested cell. The others, however, survived to create the Tudeh party immediately after Reza Shah's abdication.

May Day Parades (1941–53)

In the twelve years between the fall of Reza Shah and the creation of Mohammad Reza Shah's autocracy, May Days often took the form of mass street rallies—whenever, that is, the political authorities allowed it. These events had become mass celebrations in part because the radical intelligentsia had grown much larger and in part because Reza Shah's industrialization policies had greatly increased the ranks of the urban proletariat. By 1941 the country had 146 large factories, including 36 textile mills, 8 sugar refineries, and 8 chemical enterprises.[21]

The May Day parades were organized by the Tudeh party and its ally, the CCFTU, which had announced its reestablishment on May Day 1944 and set up headquarters in the former Socialist party building, which it renamed May First Club. In 1946–47 the CCFTU boasted 180 unions with over 300,000 members. These figures are probably inflated, but the CCFTU did have branches in all large factories and modern installations, in many small factories, and even in some bazaar workshops. According to the British labor attaché in Tehran, the CCFTU claimed 45,000 oil workers, 45,000 construction laborers, 40,000 mill hands, 20,000 railwaymen, 20,000 carpet weavers, 11,000 dockworkers, 9,000 shoemakers, 9,000 food processors, 8,000 miners, 8,000 tobacco cleaners, 6,000 truck and taxi drivers, 5,000 fishery workers, 3,500 employees in the Education Ministry, 3,000 slaughterhouse workers, 3,000 brewers, 3,000 munitions workers, 3,000 cart drivers, 3,000 sugar refiners, 2,700 hospital attendants, 2,300 chemical workers, 2,000 printers, 2,000 glassmakers, 2,000 cotton cleaners, 2,000 silk workers, 1,500 bath attendants, 1,200 cement workers, 1,000 engineers and technicians, 600 electricians, and 150 newspaper sellers.[22] The CCFTU also had affiliates in nonindustrial employments where Armenians and Assyrians were well represented: carpenters, pharmacists, cinema attendants, and pastry cooks.

The Tudeh organized its largest May Day celebration in 1946. Huge street rallies marked the end of World War II and demonstrated the strength of the labor movement. On the eve of the celebration, the government, pressured by the Tudeh, announced a one-day paid holiday, even though May Day fell on a Wednesday. At 7 A.M. workers from the major factories in Tehran, most of which were near the railroad station in the southwest of the city, began to march to the CCFTU headquarters near Ferdowsi Square in northern Tehran. They had music bands, union signs, and banners declaring "Factory Owners, the Workers Have

Awakened" and "Bread, Work, and Health for All." At the CCFTU headquarters they were met by students marching from the university in the northwest. *Zafar* (Victory), the CCFTU organ, claimed that the festivities involved some 80,000 people, making it the largest May Day parade thus far not only in Iran but in the whole of the Middle East.[23] According to one reporter, the streets were full of men, women, and children, some wearing red carnations, listening to music, watching puppet shows and folk dances, and in some places doing the foxtrot.[24] According to Donald Wilber, the well-known art historian and American undercover agent, the most impressive of the marching contingents was the Union of Dry Cleaners. "I am certain," he wrote, "that they were wearing their customers' suits; at least one suit looked very like one belonging to a man in the Legation."[25]

The festivities concluded at 2 P.M. with a factory worker reciting a poem, a representative of the main left-wing women's organization reading a message, and the head of the CCFTU honoring those killed in Reza Shah's prisons and reading off a list of union demands. The list included equal pay for men and women, work for the unemployed, housing for the homeless, support for the Republican cause in Spain, and, most important of all, a labor law that would guarantee an eight-hour day, recognize trade unions, and accept May Day as a public holiday.

There were similar celebrations in every provincial capital and in such smaller towns as Qom, Kerman, Rafsanjan, Mallayer, Ardekan, Arak, and Nain. In some places, the unions held their rally at the local football field.[26] In Abadan, where the oil company had declared a paid holiday, the parade was three miles long and probably as large as in Tehran. Its banners were in Persian, Arabic, Armenian, Assyrian, and Hindi, reflecting the ethnic composition of the oil workers. The organizers, some of them veterans of the 1929 May Day strike, demanded better housing, a minimum wage, improved rations, union recognition, and a labor law. According to a British report, the union leaders were mostly "drivers, fitters, and plant attendants."[27] The parades in Abadan and the oil region were so impressive that the British consul in Ahwaz reported that the "effective government of the province was in the hands of the Tudeh."[28] Meanwhile, a British colonel in charge of security in the oil regions was warning London that the May Day parades had proved that the "Tudeh were masters of the situation," that the safety of the refinery and oil fields as well as of British personnel depended on "the goodwill and pleasure of the Tudeh Party," and that its mass meetings were increasingly targeting the British—in one such rally a woman speaker accused the company of plundering the country's resources and called for the prompt nationalization of the whole oil industry.[29] This was probably the first time the call for oil nationalization had been heard in the streets of Iran. The British—repeating their 1929 actions—anchored two warships off Abadan, reinforced their base at Basra, and drew up contingency plans for military invasion of Khuzestan.[30]

In the coverage of the 1946 May Day, the Tudeh press printed pictures not only of large crowds but also of women participants, some veiled, others not; of men wearing cloth caps; and of the Iranian flag displayed prominently near the main speakers. All the parades were peaceful except in Kermanshah, where the police attacked workers as they came out of a cinema showing a Soviet film. Six workers were killed, becoming the first May Day martyrs in Iran. Even though these rallies did not substantiate CCFTU's inflated membership claims, they did show that the labor movement was a force to be reckoned with—so much so that two weeks later the government decreed the country's first comprehensive Labor Law, which was quickly shelved as soon as royal autocracy was reestablished.

May Day under Autocracy (1953–78)

The memory of the mass festivals survived, especially among the older generation of industrial workers, despite government repression and the dramatic social changes of the 1960s and 1970s. Immediately after the 1953 coup, the regime banned May Day meetings and effectively dismantled the whole Tudeh party, especially its labor unions. It created government syndicates, which, unlike trade unions, were confined to individual factories, and placed paid informers in large industrial installations—even the tsarist police had not been able to afford to set up such an extensive spy apparatus.[31] May Days were observed only in prison,[32] in private homes under the guise of weddings and family celebrations,[33] in factories where leftists had managed to get elected into the government syndicates,[34] and in exile, where leftist papers, irrespective of organizational affiliations, scrupulously observed the occasion. In fact, the observance of May Day distinguished leftist papers from others.

Industrialization produced a new generation of factory workers. By the mid-1970s, Iran had over 900 large and medium-sized factories, employing nearly 270,000 workers.[35] These included new textile plants in Isfahan, Tehran, Kashan, Behshahr, and Kermanshah; steel mills in Isfahan and Ahwaz; additional oil refineries in Shiraz, Tabriz, Qom, Tehran, and Kermanshah; shoe factories in Tehran, Tabriz, and Isfahan; petrochemical plants in Abadan, Shiraz, and Kharg Island; machine-tool factories in Tabriz, Arak, and Abadan; aluminum smelters in Saveh, Ahwaz, and Arak; assembly plants for cars, tractors, and trucks in Saveh, Tehran, Arak, and Tabriz; and food- and beverage-processing plants in many of the large urban centers. Nearly half of these factories were located in the Tehran region—most of them in the city's western, southern, and eastern suburbs. If one includes wage earners in oil, transport, lumber, docks, mines, and fisheries, the modern working class reached half a million. About 20 percent of the workers in the large factories were enrolled in government syndicates; but a secret 1973 survey showed that even they had little faith in these syndicates.[36]

These years also saw a massive influx of landless peasants into the cities. They outnumbered not only the older but also the newer generation of industrial workers. In fact, urbanization outpaced industrialization, producing sprawling slums, shantytowns, and squatter settlements—most of them without teahouses and coffeehouses, which served as social centers for male workers. Between 1956 and 1977, Tehran grew from 1,512,000 to 4,500,000; Isfahan, from 254,000 to 670,000; Mashad, from 241,000 to

670,000; Shiraz, from 170,000 to 416,000; and Qom, from 96,000 to 246,000.[37] By 1976, nearly half the country's population resided in urban centers. The migrants who did not find employment in the new factories tried to make ends meet by working as street peddlers, household servants, or unskilled day laborers, especially in the construction industry.[38]

Nevertheless, the memory of May Day survived, because government newspapers reported such celebrations in other countries, underground leftist papers commemorated the day, and so many had actively participated in the 1941–53 mass rallies. The regime, which had promised a national holiday honoring workers in its Labor Law, began in the mid-1970s to openly observe May Day.[39] It needed the support of the expanding industrial proletariat to oppose the dramatic emergence of the Mojahedin and Fedayin guerrillas, and it wanted to neutralize repercussions from a violent May Day confrontation that took place in 1971 between police and striking workers at the large Chit-e Jahan cotton mill in Karaj (Karaj, originally a separate village west of Tehran, was fast becoming an industrial suburb of the capital).

In the early 1970s, the shah drastically expanded the state-controlled syndicates, placing them under the new Resurgence party, giving them a newspaper, decreeing improvements in the Labor Law, and substantially increasing real wages—those for skilled workers rose by as much as 22 percent.[40] He also began to mark May Day. On May Day 1974, he addressed four thousand "syndicate representatives" who had been bused to Sa^{C}adabad Palace. He promised them houses, factory shares, a workers' holiday, and "justice against exploiting employers."[41] On May Day 1975, the Resurgence party convened a nationwide congress which gave prominence to workers' issues.[42] In the same week, the crown prince held a special audience in Niavaran Palace to award medals to young model workers.[43] On May Day 1976, the shah promised a higher standard of living to a Congress of Syndicates convened at the main Tehran sports stadium.[44] Similarly, on May Day 1977, the shah decreed that the Labor Law would be extended to small factories and bazaar workshops, which previous labor laws had not covered.[45]

May Day in 1979

The Khomeinists, despite their populist rhetoric, initially paid lit-tle attention to May Day. In fact, they were caught off guard when they discovered in late April 1979 that the leftist parties were making major preparations for the occasion.[46] Not to be outdone, the Islamic Republican party (IRP)—at the time, the main nucleus of the Khomeinists—rushed at the last minute to organize its own May Day rally. To help, the government upped the minimum wage and declared the day to be a paid public holiday. Khomeini broadcast a resounding May Day speech warning workers to be-ware of nonbelievers and proclaiming that their true guardian was Islam. "Every day should be considered Workers' Day for labor is the source of all things, even of heaven and hell as well as of the atom particle."[47] This sounded more radical than the Marxist labor theory of value.

On the eve of May Day, all the major newspapers, including those of the IRP, carried special articles on the working class. These invariably included histories of May Day, beginning with Haymarket, continuing with the Second International, and end-ing with the 1941–53 mass rallies. Most discussed the rallies with-out mentioning the Tudeh. Some exaggerated the size and mili-tancy of these rallies, claiming that they would have culminated in a successful revolution if it had not been for their organizers' "reformist" character.

Early in the morning, four separate rallies began to assemble in Tehran. The IRP marched to Imam Hosayn Square in the city's northeast district from Railway Square and Shush Square near the southern slums, from Revolution Square near Tehran University in the west, and from the industrial districts of Narmak in the east. According to an anticlerical newspaper the procession from Revo-lution Square to Imam Hosayn Square alone was three kilometers long.[48] The rally was cosponsored by the IRP-dominated factory councils and the Society of Tehran Clerics. The sponsors warned demonstrators to carry only the official *plakard*s (placards), which proclaimed that "Every Day Is Workers' Day."[49] The meet-ing ended with speeches by a Palestinian Liberation Organization delegate, by Ayatollah Beheshti, the IRP leader, and by Abul-Hosayn Banisadr, then one of Khomeini's closest advisers.

Meanwhile, a coalition of leftist groups headed by the Fedayin and the Maoist Paykar marched to Ferdowsi Square from Workers' House near the Parliament building in downtown Tehran. Workers' House was a social center that had been taken over by the Paykar during the revolution. According to a paper sympathetic to this rally, the procession had half a million participants.[50]

The Tudeh marched in midtown from Army Square to Shimran Gate, where they heard a speech by a tobacco worker and a message from the Communist-dominated trade unions in France. This rally was cosponsored by twenty-three syndicates, some of which were new, whereas others were government syndicates taken over by the Tudeh. After the Shimran Gate meeting, some of the Tudeh demonstrators went to the IRP rally in the nearby Imam Hosayn Square. Some of their banners were in Azerbayjani Turkish as well as in Persian. Eric Rouleau of *Le monde* wrote that nearly half the trade unions in Tehran supported the Tudeh rally.[51] Another foreign observer, although critical of the Tudeh for preferring traditional unions to grass-roots factory councils, admitted that the Tudeh probably had more support among factory workers than the other leftist organizations.[52]

The Mojahedin held their own rally in the Agricultural College in Karaj, where the group had formed in secret in the mid-1960s. The rally was addressed by labor organizers who had participated in the May 1971 bloody confrontation at the Chit-e Jahan mill. The Mojahedin now dominated the workers' council at that mill.[53] In addition to political demands, the Karaj rally called for decent wages, a proper labor law, and equal pay for men and women for equal work.

The Iranian press, closely scrutinized by the authorities, did not dare to compare the sizes of the four rallies, but Eric Rouleau reported that they were of equal size and each had "several hundred thousand" participants.[54] The *New York Times*, however, estimated that the IRP drew 30,000 while the Tudeh and the other leftist rallies within Tehran together had approximately 100,000 participants.[55] What is certain is that they were the largest May Day parades ever held in Tehran.

The four rallies addressed common themes: the importance of May Day and the need for a more progressive labor law that would guarantee Workers' Day, independent unions, the right to strike, the eight-hour day, the forty-hour week, and equal pay for equal work (even the clerical IRP demanded that women should get the same pay as men). All four paid allegiance to the Islamic Republic headed by Imam Khomeini, called for more nationalization of large enterprises, and advocated militant vigilance against the imperial powers, especially the United States. IRP posters even included clenched fists and red flowers, which in the past had been associated with the Tudeh party. Some banners were in Turkish, reflecting the Azerbayjani background of many workers in Tehran.[56]

Despite the similarities, however, there were important differences, some subtle, others not so subtle. The Mojahedin, as well as the IRP, used religious imagery and the terms *mostazafin* and *kargar*. The IRP's main slogans were "Workers, Toilers, Islam Is for You"; "Workers, Today Is Your Day"; "Communists Are Imperialist Agents"; "Fraternity, Equality, and Imam Ali's Authority"; and "Our Party Is That of Allah, Our Leader Is Ruhollah [Khomeini]." Its posters depicted minarets as well as industrial machinery and red flowers (these flowers tended to be roses rather than the carnations preferred by the secular organizations). The Mojahedin's main theme for the day was that true Islam would bring about "a classless society" *(nezam-e tawhidi)*.

On the other hand, the Tudeh and other secular leftists used only nonreligious symbols and language. They welcomed unveiled women, demanded "land for the tiller," talked more in terms of class and capitalism, and described the occasion as a festival *(ᶜayd)* and celebration *(jashn)* rather than as a solemn ceremony *(marasm)*. Their banners appealed to "the workers of the world," not just to "workers." Their posters featured broken chains, the color red (flags, stars, and carnations), and unveiled female workers as well as brawny male proletarians with felt caps. The Fedayin posters showed the planetary system, to represent science as well as universal humanity, and the rising sun, as a symbol of a new age, a symbol appropriated from the nineteenth-century labor movement in Europe. The Tudeh revived its 1940s slogan "Bread for All, Education for All, and Health Care for All." Workers' House emphasized the rights of those without work, demanding unemployment benefits as well as programs to create jobs. The secular left papers published poems full of Marxist imagery: Lenin, red flags, October revolutions, the dawn of a new industrial age, and "International Workers' Solidarity."[57]

May Day rallies were also held in almost every large town, including Abadan, Isfahan, Tabriz, Ahwaz, Qazvin, Shiraz, Yazd, Arak, Sanandaj, Hamadan, and Ardabel. Hojjat al-Islam Rafsanjani addressed the Abadan rally, which was packed with oil workers. No lives were lost in these rallies although in a number of places religious vigilantes known as hezbollahis attacked the leftists, a sign of things to come.[58] Even more ominous, at the end of the day, Forqan (truth)—an underground group composed of Shariati's militant admirers—assassinated Ayatollah Motahhari, one of Khomeini's closest advisers. This was to have significant repercussions for future May Days.

May Day in 1980

May Day, 1980, was in many ways a repeat performance of the previous year—with the important difference that it came in the midst of the American-hostage crisis. As the day approached, the government declared it a public holiday, increased the minimum wage and the housing allowance for workers, and rescheduled the forthcoming parliamentary elections so as not to disrupt the occasion. Newspapers associated with the regime published special Workers' Day articles. One such article claimed that the first May Day parade had been held in San Francisco, "anti-imperialism" should be the occasion's main theme, and the Islamic Revolution had shown the whole world that imperialism could be defeated by the "workers, peasants, office employees, and bazaar merchants."[59] Khomeini made another resounding speech honoring

Plate 1. May Day poster issued by the Islamic Republican party in 1980.
Courtesy of the Hoover Institution.

Plate 2.   May Day poster issued by the Islamic Republican party in 1980.
The inscription promises workers happiness in this and the next world.
Courtesy of the Hoover Institution.

Plate 3.   May Day poster issued by the Islamic Republican party in 1980.
The inscription declares that such hands will never go to hell. Courtesy of
the Hoover Institution.

Plate 4.   May Day poster issued by the Mojahedin in 1980. Courtesy of the Hoover Institution.

"Workers' Day." He described workers as the "beacon of humanity," praised them as the "most valuable class in society," congratulated them for producing so many revolutionary martyrs, and exhorted them to stand firm against all forms of imperialism.[60]

At midmorning, the IRP convened a huge crowd outside the former U.S. Embassy, now referred to as the "American spy den." The crowd converged from the industrial suburbs of the capital: from Railway, Shush, and Khurasan Squares in the south; from Imam Hosayn Square in the northeast; from Liberation and Revolution Squares in the west; from Imamzadeh Bridge in the northwest; and from Workers' House in downtown Tehran (Workers' House had been taken over by the IRP and its Islamic councils during the previous year).

The IRP slogans and banners affirmed allegiance to the Islamic Republic and Imam Khomeini. They condemned China and the Soviet Union as well as Britain and the United States for their "imperialistic policies." They also demanded the nationalization of foreign trade and the passage of a labor law, exhorted workers to higher productivity, and denounced strikes as "antirevolutionary sabotage." An IRP leader addressing the crowd warned that America was plotting to overthrow the Islamic Republic with the help of royalist officers and "pseudoleftist" university intellectuals: "Those who incite workers to strike are American leftists."[61] He declared that May 1 should be observed not just as Workers' Day but also as Teachers' Day in honor of Ayatollah Motahhari. The rally ended by affirming support for the struggles of the world's oppressed against their imperialist oppressors. *Jomhuriye Islami*, the IRP organ, carried the headline "Iranian Workers Chant 'Oppressed of the World Unite against the Oppressors!' "

Later the same day, the Tudeh organized its own march from Army Square (now renamed Imam Khomeini Square) to the American Embassy. The rally was cosponsored by sixty-two syndicates and workers' councils. In addition to reaffirming their support for the Islamic Republic and Imam Khomeini, their slogans repeated the previous year's demands for social reforms, including land reform, equal pay for equal work, and a new labor law.

Figure 6. May Day poster issued by the Tudeh party in 1980. Courtesy of the Hoover Institution.

به‌مناسبت جشنِ جهانی کارگری اول ماه مه ۱۹۸۰
(۱۱ اردیبهشت ۱۳۵۹)

Figure 7. May Day logo issued by the Tudeh party in 1980. The inscription in Persian and Turkish calls for working-class solidarity.

They also introduced such chants as "Liberals Are American Collaborators," "Worker Participation in Factory Management," and "Abu Zarr, the Enemy of Capitalism" (Abu Zarr was one of Prophet Mohammad's companions who had denounced the opulence of the early caliphs). Even though religious themes had seeped in, the Tudeh again had unveiled women in its procession.[62] It is significant that *Mardom*, the Tudeh newspaper, in its special Labor Day issue, stressed that May Day celebrated the rights of women, as well as men, to organize effective trade unions. It also reprinted pictures of unveiled women demonstrators from previous May Days, especially from 1979, 1953, and 1946.[63] Such photographs would not have gone unnoticed by the clerics.

In addition to these rallies outside the American Embassy, other groups had their own May Day meetings. The Fedayin gathered in the vast Liberation Square, where organized hezbollahis—

Figure 8.   May Day picture issued by the Tudeh party in 1981.

brought in by trucks, probably by the authorities—threw stones at
them. Paykar met near Tehran University. The Mojahedin convened south of Railroad Square, where they were attacked by
hezbollahis on motorbikes. Rajavi, the Mojahedin leader, had to
cancel his appearance because of a death threat. Even the middle-
class National Front held a small May Day meeting on Workers'
Avenue in eastern Tehran.[64]

May Day in 1981–91

Since 1980 the Islamic Republic has done its best to tame May Day
by monopolizing, containing, sanitizing, and minimizing it. May
Days are still being observed in the early 1990s, but their form and
content have dramatically changed.

Figure 9.   May Day picture issued by the Tudeh party in 1979.

The Islamic Republic has monopolized the holiday by systematically eliminating all political opponents. In 1980 it banned Paykar, and in 1981 it outlawed the Mojahedin, the National Front, and many Marxist groups, including the Minority Fedayin (this faction, unlike the Majority Fedayin, had openly criticized the regime). In 1982 the authorities carried out mass arrests of both the Tudeh and the Majority Fedayin—two organizations that hoped to function as the regime's loyal oppositions. In fact, their May Day rallies of that year, although larger than their previous ones, had scrupulously avoided any direct criticism of the regime.[65] It is no accident that the authorities chose May 1, 1983, on which to broadcast the Tudeh leader's previously made videotape in which he "confessed" to "spying for the Soviet Union," "conspiring against Imam Khomeini," and being "insincere in his support for the Islamic Republic."[66] Finally, in 1987, when the IRP dissolved itself (mainly because of differences between conservatives and radical populists), Workers' House and its Islamic

Figure 10.   May Day
stamp (1982).

councils took over the task of holding annual May Day meetings. In some years, they have been helped by armed volunteers—especially by the Revolutionary Guards.

The regime has contained May Day by moving the event from the streets into confined spaces—first into public squares and university campuses; then into sports stadiums, as in the days of the shah; and finally, after Khomeini's death, into his large, covered mausoleum. The earlier events were processions and happy celebrations in which workers actively participated in flexing their political muscle. The later ones were solemn and tightly controlled shows in which the workers were bused in by the Revolutionary Guards to passively listen to government officials. The former reflected the influence of society over the state; the latter reflected the power of the state over society.

The regime has sanitized May Day in a number of ways. It has increasingly labeled it Workers' and Teachers' Day, giving added prominence to Motahhari's martyrdom. It has eliminated the more radical demands: the right to strike, equal pay for equal work, and the nationalization of foreign trade and large enterprises. By the late 1980s the predominant theme was the need to mobilize the population against ''American imperialism and Iraqi

Figure 11. Stamps for Workers-Teachers' Day (1987). The teachers' stamp depicts Ayatollah Motahhari.

fascism," although the importance of raising literacy and "spirituality" among the working class was also acknowledged. The only radical demand left was the need for a new labor law. In addition, some government spokesmen have claimed that the Marxists have intentionally ignored the importance of religion to nineteenth-century American labor organizers.[67] Government newspapers have given a religious coloring to the early May Days in America by translating the Knights of Labor as the Pasdaran-e Kar (Guardians of Labor).[68]

The regime has also done its best to minimize the importance of May Day. The official calendar ignores the day even though it enumerates over thirty public holidays, including Ramazan, Moharram, the Iranian New Year, the birthdays of the Prophet Mohammad and Imam Sadeq, and the anniversaries of the Islamic Republic, the Islamic Revolution, and the 1963 June Uprising. Some prominent clerics have suggested that Workers' Day should be moved to coincide with the birthday of the Hidden Imam (Mahdi).[69] By the late 1980s May Day meetings were being held in the late afternoon so that factories would not lose working hours. Government papers have drastically cut their coverage. In the early 1980s they had allocated most of their front pages for the occasion and issued special supplements. By the late 1980s they were printing no more than brief inside stories and, in some years, allocating more space to Motahhari than to Workers' Day.[70] Also, the regime has tended to organize May Days only in the capital.

The decline in the importance of May Day can be clearly traced in official pronouncements. Khomeini made his last May Day speech in 1982. In it, he hailed workers and peasants as the "country's two strong arms"; described the Prophet Mohammad and Imams Ali, Sadeq, and Baqer as hardworking "manual laborers"; and noted that the Prophet had respected physical work so much that he had kissed the calloused hands of poor toilers.[71] He repeated an old hadith in which the Prophet had declared, "The sweat of a laborer is as valuable [in the eyes of God] as the blood of the martyr." He also drew sharp distinctions between manual laborers, who enjoyed "physical" and "spiritual" happiness because of their hard work and frugality, and "capitalists," who lived in moral and corporal "sin" because of sloth, boredom, gluttony, and oversleeping. "One day in the life of a worker is more valuable than the whole life of a capitalist." This was probably the most populist of all his speeches. By the mid-1980s, however, Khomeini was leaving May Day speeches to his president and prime minister, and by the late 1980s the president and prime minister were delegating them to the labor minister and the chairman of Workers' House.

The metamorphoses of the event can be seen best in 1990. The May Day meeting was held inside Khomeini's mausoleum in the afternoon. The participants, mostly male workers, were bused in from their factories. The audience did not participate but sat listening to a series of official speeches. They cheered at the appropriate places, especially when one of the speakers declared, "God is a worker." The speakers sprinkled their talks with the fatalistic term *inshallah* (God willing). At the end of the meeting, the audience endorsed by public acclamation resolutions that reaffirmed support for the Islamic Republic, promised an increase in productivity, and asserted the need for work projects, unemployment benefits, literacy programs, and, most significant of all, the passage of the long-awaited labor law. The fact that the Islamic Republic, even after eleven years, still had no labor law indicated the nature of the regime's populism: a great deal of radical rhetoric but little concrete action in terms of improving workers' living conditions. Even radical symbols had been drained of their potency: instead of the simple but vibrant red carnation, the official newspapers carried pictures of vased and elaborate bouquets— the type found in funeral parlors and bourgeois homes. That evening a Workers' Theater Group performed a play entitled *Every Day Is Like Every Other Day*. May Day had been tamed. But the fact that it has survived, even in this tamed form, reflects the symbolic strength of the leftist tradition in modern Iran.

4

History Used and Abused

We owe everything to the clergy. History
shows that in the past millennium it was
always the clergy who led the popular and
revolutionary movements. It was the clergy
who always produced the first martyrs. It was
the clergy who always defended the oppressed
against the money worshipers.

Ayatollah Khomeini, speech, Ettela^{c}at,
1 March 1989

While in prison in the last few months I have
had the opportunity to study history, especially
that of the Iranian Left. . . . I would like to
share my conclusion with the public,
particularly the youth, so that they will not be
led astray.

*First secretary of the Tudeh party, television
confession,* Ettela^{c}at, *28 August 1983*

History Recanted

On the eve of May Day 1983, Iranian television sprung a surprise
on its viewers. It paraded veteran Tudeh leaders confessing to a
host of major crimes, including that of advocating an "alien ideology."[1] Public confessions in themselves were nothing new. Ever
since 1981 a diverse array of political dissidents—Maoists, Mosaddeqists, former Khomeinists, royalists, and Mojahedin acti-

vists—had admitted to hatching "sinister conspiracies" and establishing "treasonable ties with foreign powers." Nor was the content of the Tudeh confessions entirely novel, for the Left had long been accused of "conspiring" to destroy the nation, disseminating "alien" concepts, and, most frequently of all, "spying" for the Soviet Union.

The surprise in these 1983 confessions, which continued intermittently for over ten months, was the prominence given to history. History featured in the recantations made by the three most important Tudeh figures: Nuraldin Kianuri, the seventy-one-year-old first secretary of the party; Ehsan Tabari, the organization's main theoretician since the mid-1940s; and Mahmud Behazin, a well-known author and fellow-traveler since the early 1940s. Behazin kicked off the first show with a lesson on the Islamic clergy's true understanding of the past, Marxism's misinterpretation of the course of history, and secular radicals' betrayal of the people of Iran through their "alien" ideology.

The three Tudeh leaders followed similar scripts. They began by greeting "Imam Khomeini, the Great Leader of the Revolution and Founder of the Islamic Republic." They stressed that their brief confinement in prison had provided them with the opportunity to study the past. Kianuri concluded his second long recantation by stressing that the Left needed to examine in great detail Iran's history and society. Tabari exclaimed that he had realized that his whole life's work was "spurious" as soon as the prison authorities introduced him to Islamic authors, notably Ayatollah Motahhari. Tabari explained that his own publications were useless because they had relied on foreign sources (Europeans, Zionists, Freemasons, and Soviet Marxists) and on Kasravi and Sangalaji, whose errors he recognized in prison as soon as he read Imam Khomeini's *Kashf al-Asrar*. A less important Tudeh leader, before being executed, limited his defense to thanking his jailers for turning the prison into a "university."

The Tudeh leaders all declared they wished to reveal their mistakes so that the younger generation would learn from them. Tabari, for instance, warned the youth that Marxism would inevitably cut them off from their own people, history, and culture.

Figure 12.   Stamps (1983) honoring the forerunners of the Islamic Revolution. The stamps depict *(from left to right)* Shaykh Fazlollah Nuri, Ayatollah Modarres, Kuchek Khan, and Navab Safavi.

The Tudeh leaders praised the clergy for having heroically led the people throughout history, Behazin claiming that the clergy had enjoyed close links with the oppressed for over one thousand years. Kianuri stated that Marxism had no chance against the clergy since the latter were armed not only with "militant Islam" but also with age-old popular support. Moreover, they all argued that their "foreign ideology" had led them to "depend" on the Soviets, hatch conspiracies, misunderstand their own society, worship the intelligentsia, and disrespect the country's religious culture. In his first television appearance, Kianuri traced the source of "all our mistakes to our foreign ideology." In his later appearances, he no longer spoke of "mistakes" but of "illnesses," "sins," and "high treason."

Even more significant, the Tudeh leaders each cited the same four decisive points in history in which the Left had supposedly betrayed Iran: the Constitutional Revolution, especially the government's forceful disarming of Sattar Khan's fighters in 1910; the Jangali (Jungle) Resistance of 1915–21, ending with the death of its leader, Mirza Kuchek Khan, in the wooded mountains of

Gilan; the rise of Reza Shah in 1921–25, particularly the opposition to his coronation mustered by Ayatollah Modarres; and Mosaddeq's 1951–53 administration, terminating with his overthrow in the notorious August 19 coup. Since the 1983 television confessions, these four crises have featured prominently in government propaganda: in newspapers, radio broadcasts, Friday sermons, school textbooks, and even intellectual journals. Government officials sometimes cite these Tudeh recantations to prove their case. The Islamic Republic has certainly not treated history as bunk. Indeed, it has gone to considerable trouble—with somewhat unconventional means—to obtain the "historical truth."

This chapter has three interconnected aims. The first is to describe how the regime has used these four crises as "defining moments" in which the Left "betrayed" the nation whereas the clergy valiantly resisted imperialism, feudalism, and despotism. It will therefore explore which aspects of the crises are highlighted, minimized, or even totally overlooked.

The second aim is to show how the regime tries to use history to give itself populistic as well as religious legitimacy. Whereas Khomeini (at least, in his theological treatises) used holy texts to support the clergy's right to rule, the Islamic Republic claims the same right on the grounds that the clergy have valiantly saved the country from imperialism, feudalism, and despotism. This is legitimacy based not so much on divine right as on the secular function of preserving national independence.

The third aim is to demonstrate that the regime's propaganda is designed not only to marginalize leftists but also to co-opt non-religious nationalists—namely, the Mosaddeqists. In Iranian historiography, these four landmark crises are highly controversial precisely because they have appeared to separate prominent "nationalists" from equally prominent "leftists": Sattar Khan, the "savior" of the Constitutional Revolution, from the secular Social Democrats and Yeprem Khan, the Armenian guerrilla turned police chief; Kuchek Khan, the Jangali, from Haydar Khan, the Communist party head; Ayatollah Modarres from Suleyman Iskandari, the Socialist party founder; and, of course, Mosaddeq from Kianuri and the other Tudeh leaders. It should also be noted that the Islamic Republic—like most governments that appeal to the lowest common denominator—does its best to reduce complex ideological issues to simple personality conflicts in which one side epitomizes goodness, the other wickedness.

The Constitutional Revolution (1905–10)

The Constitutional Revolution began in 1905 as a broad-based urban movement led by the three most important senior clerics in Tehran: Sayyid Abdollah Behbehani, Sayyid Mohammad Tabatabai, and Shaykh Fazlollah Nuri. But the movement eventually broke apart. First, Shaykh Nuri defected to the royalists in 1908, enabling the shah to bomb Parliament and execute some of the revolutionaries. This triggered off the civil war of 1908–9. In changing sides, Shaykh Nuri accused his former colleagues of imitating foreigners, subverting the sacred law, being secret Babis (forerunners of Bahais) and Freemasons, and introducing hereti-

cal notions such as liberty, equality, anarchism, nihilism, socialism, and "naturalism" (the supremacy of natural law over divine
law).[2] He excommunicated the leading constitutionalists on the
grounds they were apostates and "sowers of corruption on
earth"—both capital offenses according to the sacred law.[3] After
the civil war, Shaykh Nuri himself was hanged for "sowing corruption on earth."

A further split occurred in 1910 when a group of guerrilla
fighters headed by Sattar Khan, a hero of the civil war, refused to
obey a government order to disarm. After a brief but violent
confrontation at Atabek Park in Tehran, Yeprem Khan, the recently appointed police chief, succeeded in disarming them. Yeprem Khan used Bakhtiyari tribesmen as well as fellow Armenian
veterans of the civil war. He also received the support of a radical
named Haydar Khan, who had recently helped found the secular
Democrat party.[4] After the Atabek Park incident, Sattar Khan,
who was wounded in the confrontation, was pensioned off, and
his supporters were disbanded. Some hail Sattar Khan as the real
hero of the Constitutional Revolution, crediting him with saving
Tabriz during the civil war and trying to prevent the revolutionary
movement from being disarmed. They also describe him as a
"martyr," claiming that his death, four years later, was caused by
wounds sustained at Atabek Park.

The Khomeinists, including Khomeini himself, have not always
been consistent in their evaluations of the Constitutional Revolution. At times, especially in their prepopulist days, they depicted
the revolution, from its very inception, as a wholly British "plot"
hatched in their legation, carried out by their "agents" (*ᶜummal*),
and designed to undermine the sacred law.[5] At other times, especially at the height of their populist rhetoric, they have praised the
revolution as a mass anti-imperialist struggle that had initially
been led by the clergy but had later been taken over by scheming
secular radicals.[6] "The constitutional movement," Khomeini argued, "started well, but in time corrupt individuals took it over
and thereby alienated the public."[7] One of Khomeini's close advisers claimed that leftists began to betray the country as early as
1909 when troublemakers from the Caucasus sowed dissension

among the clergy, causing Shaykh Nuri's martyrdom and Ayatollah Behbehani's assassination.[8]

In the prepopulist interpretation, Shaykh Nuri was the true
hero. Al-Ahmad, in his famous pamphlet *Gharbzadegi* (The
plague from the West), claimed that Shaykh Nuri was martyred in
front of a large jeering crowd in Cannon Square because he tried
to protect Islam from the likes of "Malkum Khan, the Armenian,
and Taliboff, the Caucasian Social Democrat." "To my mind,"
proclaimed al-Ahmad, "the corpse of that great man dangling on
the gallows is like a flag raised to signify the triumph of this deadly
disease."[9] Feraydun Adamiyat, the leading historian of the Constitutional Revolution, retorted that al-Ahmad's praise for traditional
culture and denunciation of Western ideas would inevitably lead
to the conclusion that Iran should never free itself of its traditional
institutions, including that of oriental despotism.[10]

Khomeini was equally admiring of Shaykh Nuri. He claimed
that "enemies of Islam" executed him by cleverly fooling the
public as well as the other grand ayatollahs.[11] Khomeini's disciples
have praised Shaykh Nuri as the "Islamic movement's first martyr in contemporary Iran." They have argued that Orientalists as
well as Iranian secularists conspired to smear him as a "reactionary mulla" and have said that he was executed by Armenians,
Freemasons, and others contaminated with the Western plague.[12]
One newspaper article went so far as to claim that the orders for
his execution had come directly from the British Foreign Office.[13]
It is significant that postage stamps issued by the Islamic Republic
have honored Shaykh Nuri but not Behbehani and Tabatabai.

By accepting in his television recantation the official version of
Shaykh Nuri, Kianuri added a personal dimension to the historic
crisis: Shaykh Nuri was Kianuri's grandfather. However,
Kianuri's father, Shaykh Mahdi, Nuri's eldest son, had been a
staunch revolutionary; it was even rumored that Shaykh Mahdi
had been a member of the jeering crowd at his father's execution.[14] These rumors, however, are highly suspect, for their source
was an extremely conservative British commentator who not only
sided with the tsar and the Qajars but was also eager to prove that
most Iranians, especially the constitutional liberals, were devoid

of all humane instincts, including that of family feelings.[15] Mahdi Malekzadeh, a leading historian and participant in the revolution, dismissed the whole story as pure fabrication.[16]

In the more populistic interpretation of the Constitutional Revolution, the Islamic Republic claims the real heroes of the revolution to be Ayatollahs Behbehani and Tabatabai and their ally among the armed volunteers Sattar Khan. According to this view, all was well until 1909–10, when the secular radicals of the Democrat party pushed the two grand ayatollahs aside, assassinated Behbehani, and forcefully disarmed the more devout guerrillas. This view incorporates the Constitutional Revolution into a larger picture depicting the whole of modern Iranian history—from the 1891 Tobacco Crisis to the 1979 Islamic Revolution—as a people's anti-imperialist struggle led entirely by the "freedom-loving" clergy.[17]

Both interpretations distort the Constitutional Revolution by ignoring the contributions of the other social groups: the merchants who sparked off the whole crisis, the bazaar guilds that provided the revolution with its popular base, the intellectuals whose secret societies helped coordinate the movement, the reform-minded aristocrats who weakened the establishment from within, and the Bakhtiyari tribesmen who, together with the Armenian and Georgian volunteers, did much of the decisive fighting.[18]

The mythology surrounding Shaykh Nuri obscures several awkward facts about him. Shaykh Nuri had been on good terms with the Russians since the turn of the century.[19] He had refused to support the early bazaar protests against the Europeans in charge of collecting customs dues. He had caused a major scandal in 1905 by endorsing the sale of a cemetery to the Russians for the construction of their bank—the inadvertent exhuming of bodies had triggered street protests.[20] He had organized an anticonstitutionalist rally in June 1907 after obtaining funds from the same Russian bank.[21] In breaking with Parliament, Shaykh Nuri become the main court ideologue. He praised the shah as the guardian of Islam, arguing that representative government contradicted Islam and that obedience to the monarchy was a divine obligation incumbent on all, including the clergy.[22] What is more, he endangered the lives of the leading constitutionalists by denouncing them as atheists, heretics, apostates, and secret Babis—charges designed to incite the devout to violence. In fact, Shaykh Nuri was finally condemned to death by a fellow ayatollah not so much for supporting the shah as for being responsible for the murder of leading constitutionalists. In describing Shaykh Nuri's execution, school textbooks now cite al-Ahmad's eulogy and add that the presiding judge had sold himself to the West. They also make the preposterous claim that Yeprem Khan—an Armenian with little education and absolutely no legal training—had sat on the high court that had condemned the grand ayatollah to death.[23]

Khomeini's treatment of Shaykh Nuri and the constitutionalists is somewhat disingenuous. He denounced the constitutionalists for not demanding the abolition of the monarchy but at the same time praised Shaykh Nuri for opposing the same reformers, leaving the impression that Shaykh Nuri opposed kingship.[24] In actual fact, the constitutionalists had wanted limited monarchy whereas Shaykh Nuri had argued in favor of kingship unfettered by elected assemblies. To claim Shaykh Nuri as the forerunner of the anti-monarchical movement is to turn history inside out.

The religious-populist mythology surrounding Tabatabai, Behbehani, and Sattar Khan is equally distorting. Tabatabai not only admired European liberalism but was also a not-so-secret member of the Freemason Lodge in Tehran.[25] Behbehani had kept silent during the 1891 Tobacco Crisis, and again in 1902 when the British obtained an oil concession—probably because the British had given him some "expense money."

While some hailed Sattar Khan as the savior of Tabriz and the "Garibaldi" of Iran, many fellow revolutionaries saw him as a "drunkard," "brigand," and "plunderer."[26] The government disarmed Sattar Khan not because he was a radical determined to push the revolution further—as latter-day populists would like to believe—but because it feared, with good reason, that the continued fighting between rival gangs would tax the patience of the public.[27] Sattar Khan made his last stand not over any principle but over the monetary compensation offered for his weapons.[28]

Many of his final supporters were Georgians who could not return home and whose employment prospects in Iran were bleak. He himself was affiliated with the conservative Moderate party, which was led by wealthy politicians, even former royalists. This party opposed the Democrats over social issues such as land reform, child labor, progressive income tax, women's education, and equality before the law. Finally, the description of Sattar Khan as the savior of Tabriz and the revolution conveniently overlooks the fact that Bakhtiyaris, Armenian's, and Georgians did much of the decisive fighting and that Tabriz was saved from the royalist siege thanks to the timely intervention of the Tsarist army, which Sattar Khan himself welcomed as the only alternative to famine and defeat.[29]

The Jangali Resistance (1915–21)

Mirza Kuchek Khan, the famous Sardar-e Jangal (Jungle Commander), has attracted more attention than any other personality in the history of early twentieth-century Iran. Nationalists see him as an "unyielding patriot," an "incorruptible leader," and an "indefatigable fighter" who took to the mountains of northern Iran with the burning "ambition of ridding the country" of Russian and British troops.[30] According to this interpretation, his revolution would have succeeded but for Lenin's willingness to sacrifice Iran to reach a compromise with Britain.[31] For local reformers, Kuchek Khan fought for regional autonomy as well as against feudal landlords and corrupt tribal chiefs.[32] For some leftists, he was a Che Guevara, the forests of Gilan were the Sierra Maestra, his bearded followers were revolutionary peasants, and his short-lived Soviet Socialist Republic was a forerunner of revolutionary Cuba.

For Khomeinists, Kuchek Khan was a turbaned martyr who raised the banner of Islam against the West and died fighting both the monarchists and the Communists.[33] He froze to death in the Gilan highlands because of "Communist intrigues" and because his principles would not permit him to seek asylum in the Soviet

Union.[34] The Islamic Republic has honored him with postage stamps and posters, as well as articles, books, and full chapters in school textbooks. It has also funded a fourteen-hour television epic entitled *Kuchek-e Jangal.*

Even his opponents pay grudging respect to Kuchek Khan. A British officer in the military expedition sent to the Caucasus via Gilan described him as the Robin Hood of the Caspian Marches, taking from the rich to give to the poor.[35] He also described him as endowed with "courage, personal magnetism, and great force of character."[36] The governor of Gilan in the aftermath of the revolt praised him as a "brave" and "altruistic patriot."[37] Meanwhile, historians in the Soviet Union have depicted him as a well-intentioned nationalist misled into killing Haydar Khan by "reactionary advisers."[38] Kuchek Khan's admirers retort that this dramatic killing occurred either without his knowledge or as a defensive measure against a Communist plot.

The Islamic Republic's portrayal of the Jangalis is incomplete. For one thing, it overlooks the fact that Kuchek Khan was a social conservative. He fought in the constitutional movement in the entourage of a wealthy northern landlord and joined the conservative Moderate party. At times, he collaborated with the Qajars; the title of Sardar-e Jangal as well as the governorship of the Fuman district in Gilan were given to him by Ahmad Shah. At other times, he negotiated with Britain, Colonel Reza Khan, and even archconservative ministers in Tehran—though his supporters have tried to argue that he was really negotiating with more progressive members of the government.[39] In 1919 he was even willing to support the notorious Anglo-Persian Agreement. If Kuchek Khan was a rebel, it was in the tradition of Robin Hood and other "primitive" rebels.[40]

The Islamic Republic's portrayal also blows the Jangalis completely out of proportion. The movement—if it can be called that—was launched in 1915 with the assistance of the Central Powers.[41] At its height in the midst of World War I, it totaled no more than 2,000 armed men, and by 1919 it was as good as dead, able to muster no more than 500 armed men. Kuchek Khan's foreign assistance dried up, and his bookkeeper absconded with the remaining funds. His right-hand man, Dr. Heshmat (Taleqani), withdrew from politics and fell into government hands. Vossugh al-Dawleh, the pro-British premier, promptly hanged him. Kuchek Khan himself was quietly negotiating with the same premier. What revived the movement briefly in 1920 was not the controversial Anglo-Persian Agreement, as official histories claim, but the sudden arrival of the Red Army in Enzeli. The Red Army intervened not so much to help the Jangalis as to chase the White Russians and their British patrons out of the Caspian area.

The Jangali forces remained modest, and divided, even when the Red Army helped them establish the Soviet Socialist Republic of Iran in Gilan. Khomeinists refer to this government simply as the "republican government."[42] In the Soviet Socialist Republic, Kuchek Khan probably had no more than 300 armed guerrillas, many of them sons of the local gentry. Ehsanallah Khan, a militant Democrat, had about 200, most of them radical intellectuals from Tehran. Khalu Qurban, a Kurd from Kermanshah, had less than 150, all of them Kurds and Lurs from his home region. The Iranian Communist party had 300, many of them Turkish-speaking Iranians from Baku. Meanwhile, the Red Army in Gilan had over 1,000.[43] According to Gregor Yeqikian, Kuchek Khan's trusted translator, some of the Red soldiers were Armenians from Baku who had volunteered to serve in Iran because the Soviet Socialist Republic of Azerbayjan had spread rumors that Muslims in Gilan were massacring Christians.[44] Yeqikian, who was Armenian himself, categorically denied these rumors. However, relations between other ethnic groups were tense. Numerous memoirs describe how there were bad feelings between Gilanis and outsiders and between Tehranis, Kurds, and Turkish-speakers from Baku.[45]

Although Khomeinists, nationalists, and some leftists have depicted the Jangalis as a "peasant movement," none of the many primary sources provide evidence for such a claim. The rural population may have provided money and shelter, but few fighters. This is not surprising. Kuchek Khan's main financial supporters, such as Mirza Hosayn Kasma'i, were local merchants and landlords. Fuman, Kuchek Khan's base, was inhabited by Kurds and Taleshi villagers tied strongly to their feudal patron, who was hostile to Kuchek Khan and controlled more armed men than the Jangalis.[46] A 1920 Red Army report concluded that there was no such thing as a "revolutionary peasantry" in Iran.[47]

The fate of the Soviet Socialist Republic was sealed as early as the summer of 1921. Ehsanallah Khan, without consulting his colleagues, launched an ill-prepared and consequently disastrous march on Tehran. Khalu Qurban and many of Kuchek Khan's own fighters made their own peace with Reza Khan—some became his ardent henchmen. When the Red Army began to evacuate once the British agreed to withdraw from Iran,[48] Kuchek Khan went to Enzeli to persuade the Red Army to delay the withdrawal.[49] It is paradoxical that nationalists both denounce the Soviets for interfering in Iranian affairs and, at the same time, fault them for failing to provide Kuchek Khan with greater assistance.[50] Presumably the Red Army should have continued to interfere until the central government had fallen.

The Islamic Republic's portrayal also simplifies Kuchek Khan's complex relationship with the Left. Kuchek Khan welcomed the October Revolution, adopted the socialist label, obtained arms from the Soviets, and welcomed the Red Army with the "Marseillaise" and the "Internationale." He also sought Lenin's support to the very end, especially against Ehsanallah Khan, the Soviet Socialist Republic of Azerbayjan, and the Turkish-speaking Communists from Baku, whom he contemptuously referred to as "British agents," "ignoramuses," and "nonentities" masquerading as Iranian Communists.[51] His final clash with the Left came over neither religion, the veil, nor the sanctity of the family—as claimed by the Islamic Republic—but over land reform. Haydar Khan, who took over the Iranian Communist party in October 1920 with Lenin's support, was willing to drop every radical demand for the sake of a united front with Kuchek Khan except the demand for land reform. In September 1921, only fifteen months after the establishment of the Soviet Socialist Republic in Gilan, Kuchek Khan ordered Haydar Khan's assassination. Three months later, Kuchek Khan himself froze to death in the Gilan highlands. The only person who remained with him to the bitter end was a Russian revolutionary adventurer named Gauk. Official historians tend to ignore Gauk or refer to him only by his Persian nom de guerre, Houshang.[52]

The Opposition to Reza Shah (1921–41)

The Islamic Republic portrays the clergy as the main bulwark of resistance to Reza Shah, claiming that the senior clerics not only resisted his seizure of power in 1921 but also tried to stop his coronation in 1926 and consequently bore the brunt of his dictatorial reign. It argues that the Left helped Reza Shah in his machinations of 1921–25 and collaborated with his dictatorship. In drawing this picture, the Islamic Republic focuses on Ayatollah Sayyid Hasan Modarres. According to Khomeini, "Modarres remains alive as long as history is alive."[53] According to *Ettela^cat*, Modarres is the epitome of the clergy's "struggle against despotism and imperialism."[54] And according to Ibrahim Fakhrai—Kuchek Khan's main hagiographer—Modarres is an eternal symbol of the clergy's "revolutionary" war against despotism, imperialism, and feudalism.[55]

Modarres's credentials seem impeccable. He came from a clerical family in Ardakan, graduated from an Isfahan seminary, studied with prominent senior clerics in Najaf, and taught law and theology in Isfahan. He supported the Constitutional Revolution and presided over the Provincial Assembly in Isfahan. He was prominent in the Moderate party in the second and third Parliaments; in the former he spoke on behalf of the Najaf clergy, and in the latter he represented Tehran and presided over the House. He served as justice minister in the National Government of Resistance formed during World War I to oppose the Anglo-Russian occupation. He denounced the 1919 Anglo-Persian Agreement and urged others, notably Kuchek Khan, to do the same. What is more, he was imprisoned following the 1921 coup.

From 1921 until 1925, Modarres was again prominent in Parliament, heading the Moderate party and, in the final session of the fifth Parliament, leading the opposition to the change of dynasty. Forced out of politics in 1925, he survived an assassination attempt, was banished to Khorasan, and in 1938 was strangled to death on the direct orders of Reza Shah.[56] The British legation, which had no reason to like him, described him as a man much "revered by the lower classes" on account of his "simple life" and "fearless" criticism of the high and mighty, even the shah.[57] Malek al-Shu^Cara Bahar, the famous poet and author of *Tarikh-e Mukhtasar-e Ahzab-e Siyasi-ye Iran* (Short history of Iranian political parties), esteemed him as the "greatest statesman" Iran has produced in the last six hundred years.[58]

While praising Modarres, the Islamic Republic heaps scorn on Suleyman Iskandari, the founder of the Socialist party—the heir of the early Democrats and the main parliamentary counterweight to the Moderates. It depicts Iskandari as a corrupt old-time politician with foreign connections who survived the dictatorship to chair the Tudeh party. It also dwells on the fact that he was a Qajar prince—even though this aristocratic lineage had not stopped him from taking part in the Constitutional Revolution and leading the 1924 republican movement against the Qajars. In fact, during the 1909 coup his elder brother had been murdered by the royalists and pure chance had saved him from the same fate.

The official picture of 1921–25 grossly oversimplifies both the opposition to Reza Shah and Modarres's complex career. Modarres, despite his martyrdom, was a master craftsman in the art of political expediency. His Moderate party included mainly large landlords, tribal chiefs, wealthy merchants, and titled bureaucrats. He formed alliances not only with Ahmad Shah but also with old-time politicos such as Qavam al-Mulk, Qavam al-Saltaneh, Vossugh al-Dawleh, Prince Farmanfarma, and Sardar Asad Bakhtiyar—exemplars of what the Islamic Republic likes to denounce as "corrupt feudalists spreading the Western plague."

Modarres even made crucial deals with Reza Khan. In 1922 he supported Reza Khan's bid to become war minister; in return, Reza Khan exiled Sayyid Ziya, his coconspirator in the 1921 coup. In 1924 he was instrumental in electing Reza Khan premier as part of a bargain in which the latter dropped Iskandari from the cabinet and ended Iskandari's campaign to establish a republic. The British legation reported that Modarres and the Right thought that they had tied Reza Khan to their "chariot wheels." The legation went on to predict that it was really Reza Khan who had tied them to his own chariot wheels.[59]

Moreover, Modarres—despite his clerical position—spoke a secular, rather than a religious, language.[60] He based his arguments against the 1909 and 1921 coups, the 1919 Anglo-Persian Agreement, the 1924 republican movement, the 1925 change of dynasty, and even the periodic discussions of women's suffrage not so much on Islam as on the 1906–9 constitutional laws, the sovereignty of the people, and the rights of elected parliaments. His arguments had more in common with secular liberalism than religious populism. He often drew a distinction between religion and politics, a major transgression as far as the Khomeinists are concerned. He also helped Reza Shah's minister of justice draft a new legal code—Khomeini's bête noire. Bahar, in explaining his own defection from the Democrats to the Moderates, praised Modarres for resisting the temptation to exploit religion against his opponents. He added that many of Modarres's supporters in the later parliaments were like himself secularists who wanted to keep religion out of politics.[61] The Islamic Republic often quotes Bahar's praise for Modarres without mentioning the reasons why Bahar admired him so much. Nor does it mention that Bahar entered politics in 1909 as a secular Democrat and died in 1951 as the head of the Peace Partisans, a Tudeh front organization.

Even more distorting is the Islamic Republic's overall picture of the opposition to Reza Shah. Modarres's opposition to extinguishing the Qajar monarchy was by no means typical of the religious establishment. The others senior clerics either tacitly or openly supported the change of dynasty. Some participated in Reza Shah's Napoleonic-like coronation and even hoped to place the crown on his head. Nor was Modarres's martyrdom typical; he was the only senior cleric to fall victim to Reza Shah. It was the Left that provided many of the political prisoners who lost their lives in these years. What is more, Iskandari and his two Socialist colleagues were the only delegates in the 1925 Constituent Assembly not to vote for the establishment of the Pahlavi monarchy. They were promptly banned from politics.

The Islamic Republic, while detailing Modarres's activities in the final session of the fifth Parliament, prefers to ignore completely the Constituent Assembly. It does so both because of Iskandari's vote and because many clerical delegates cast their ballot in favor of Reza Shah. Among them was a certain Ayatollah Abul-Qasem Kashani, who later became prominent in Mosaddeq's movement and is now hailed as Khomeini's immediate "precursor."[62] The fact that Kashani supported the new dynasty provides food for thought as to how Khomeini would have acted if he had been senior enough to attend the Constituent Assembly.

Mosaddeq's Administration (1951–53)

Mosaddeq, although deceased since 1967, haunts the Islamic Republic. He does so because he embodied many political features the Islamic Republic admires, but few of the social ingredients it considers essential. He had an impeccable anti-Pahlavi record. He opposed the 1925 change of dynasty and, consequently, was cast out of politics for sixteen years; it was rumored that he came close to meeting the same fate as Modarres. During 1941–53, he persistently criticized the new shah's unconstitutional powers. After Mosaddeq's overthrow in the 1953 coup, he was imprisoned, released, and then once again forced into house imprisonment, where he eventually died.

Mosaddeq had an equally impeccable anti-imperialist record. He denounced the 1919 Anglo-Persian Agreement and the 1921 coup. He opposed economic capitulations in any shape or form as well as military alliances with the Great Powers. He led the 1944–45 opposition to the granting of an oil concession to the Soviet Union, and, of course, he launched the 1951 campaign to nationalize the Anglo-Iranian Oil Company. In fact, he was one of the world's very first nonaligned leaders. What is more, he challenged the British and the shah with public support. He appealed directly to the masses, often bypassing Parliament, which he denounced at one point as a "den of thieves." A prominent royalist deputy exclaimed in exasperation:

> Is our premier a statesman or a mob leader? What type of premier says "I will speak to the people" every time he faces a political problem? I always considered this man to be unsuitable for high office. But I never imagined, even in my worst nightmares, that a seventy-year-old would turn into a rabble-rouser. A man who surrounds Parliament with thugs is nothing less than a public menace.[63]

Mosaddeq was no cleric nor was he willing to use religion against his opponents. On the contrary, he was a secular humanist and a typical offspring of the French Enlightenment. His thesis, written for a law degree at Lausanne, argued in favor of fully secularizing the legal system in Iran. His speeches used imagery from Iranian history and the Constitutional Revolution, not from Shii Islam. His closest advisers were young secular nationalists, some of whom—especially those from the Iran party—could be described as militantly anticlerical. His administration contained no clerics and few technocrats with clerical connections. He was reluctant to appoint Mahdi Bazargan as minister of education, suspecting that Bazargan would bring too much religion into the schools. What is more, a small group of religious fanatics known as the Fedayan-e Islam tried to assassinate Mosaddeq and wounded Hosayn Fatemi, his foreign minister.

Unable to exorcise Mosaddeq's ghost, the Islamic Republic has tried to contain it. High school textbooks allocate twelve pages to Kuchek Khan, four pages to Modarres, another four to Shaykh Nuri, and less than two to Mosaddeq—about the same as given to Navab Safavi, the Fedayan-e Islam leader.[64] Meanwhile, the mass media elevate Ayatollah Kashani as the real leader of the oil nationalization campaign, depicting Mosaddeq as merely the ayatollah's hanger-on. Even more significant, the regime portrays the 1951–53 period as yet another example of leftist betrayal, arguing that the nationalist movement failed because it was stabbed in the back by the Tudeh.

This last theme plays well in nationalist circles precisely because it repeats the arguments the National Front has used ever since the 1953 coup. According to the National Front, Mosaddeq would have survived if the Tudeh had given him greater support, would have been able to counter the West if the Soviets had offered assistance, and would have been able to resist the coup if the Tudeh had been willing to mobilize its clandestine military network.[65] These arguments, now Mosaddeqist catechisms, contain only half-truths. It is true that the Tudeh did not support the National Front initially, but by 1953 it had moved close to Mosaddeq. The Tudeh participated in pro-Mosaddeq demonstrations, helped scotch an attempted royalist coup, and called for the establishment of a republic. It was the only large organization to support Mosaddeq's highly controversial referendum of July 1953 proposing to dissolve Parliament. By then, ten of the original twenty founding members of the National Front had defected to the royalist camp. Khomeini, like many other clerics, opposed the 1953 referendum on the avowed grounds that it violated the fundamental laws of the 1906 constitution.[66]

It is true that the Soviets did not go out of their way to help Mosaddeq, but this was as much due to the latter as the former. Mosaddeq's whole strategy was designed to obtain American support against the British. At the height of the Cold War he knew perfectly well that if he moved closer to the Soviets, he would automatically alienate the Americans. Even after the coup, he kept up the pretense that he had been overthrown not by the Americans but by the British.

It is also true that the Tudeh did not mobilize its military network to stop the coup, but again this had much to do with Mosaddeq's own decisions.[67] On August 14, Kianuri, who was then the head of the Tudeh military network, informed Mosaddeq that a coup was in the making and provided him with a list of conspirators. Mosaddeq took no notice, saying that he had appointed most of these senior officers. On August 16, the same officers seized three cabinet ministers who were most in favor of an alliance with the Tudeh. On August 18, Mosaddeq, at the urging of the American ambassador, ordered the martial law authorities to clear the streets of all demonstrators. About six hundred Tudeh supporters were arrested. Finally, on August 19, when the coup was in progress, Kianuri phoned Mosaddeq to offer help, but Mosaddeq declined the offer on the grounds that "he did not want bloodshed" and that "events were now beyond his control." It is also significant that on the eve of the coup one of the main National Front papers pronounced the royalist danger to be dead and warned that the main threat now came from the Tudeh.[68]

If Mosaddeq fell because of a "stab in the back," the stab came not so much from the Left as from the religious Right. From the very beginning, the clerical establishment had arrayed itself against the National Front. Ayatollah Behbehani, the senior cleric in Tehran and the grandson of the famous constitutional leader, had openly sided with the shah. The substantial influx of CIA money into the Tehran bazaar on the eve of the 1953 coup became known as "Behbehani dollars." Even more important, Ayatollah Borujerdi—a staunch royalist and the leading *marja^c-e taqlid* from 1944 until his death in 1961—had tried to stem Mosaddeq's popularity by issuing an edict forbidding the clergy from participating in politics. He epitomized the conservative clergy, who claimed to be apolitical but in fact bolstered the royalist regime. Ruhani, Khomeini's main biographer, tries to explain Borujerdi's behavior by claiming that the "imperialists" had planted "agents" around him to isolate him from society.[69]

Ayatollah Kashani was one of the few prominent clerics to ignore Borujerdi's ban and support Mosaddeq. The Islamic Republic makes much of Kashani's forthright rejection of the ban but takes care not to mention who issued the edict nor that Borujerdi was Khomeini's main mentor for nearly two decades.[70] Even though Kashani publicly supported Mosaddeq, their relations were problematic from the very beginning. As early as November 1951, the British Embassy reported that Kashani was so disgruntled with Mosaddeq that he had put out "feelers" in many directions, including the royal court and the U.S. Embassy. "The Americans," reported the British Embassy, "have told us in the strictest confidence that he [Kashani] has been in touch with them. His main thesis is the danger of communism and the need for immediate American aid."[71] Similarly, in May 1952 the head

Figure 13.
Stamp (1981) honoring
Ayatollah Kashani.

of the British intelligence service in Tehran reported that a prominent royalist had boasted to him that the ''shah's astute policies''
had detached Kashani from Mosaddeq. He added, ''I did not
dispute this but would put on record that the detaching of Kashani
was due to quite other factors, and that these factors were created
and directed by the brothers Rashidian.''[72] (The Rashidian brothers were the main conduit of British intelligence service money
into Iran.)[73]

Kashani's opposition to Mosaddeq came into the open by mid-
1953 once the latter issued a referendum to dissolve Parliament,
drafted an electoral bill enfranchising women, tended to favor
state enterprises over the bazaar, refused to ban alcohol, and
declined amnesty to assassins from the Fedayan-e Islam. More
mundane matters, such as the awarding of government contracts,
also played a role. According to British intelligence, Kashani's two
sons had set up a lucrative business buying and selling import
licenses for prohibited goods using their father's threats.[74] At this
time Kashani also suddenly discovered that Mosaddeq's thesis,
written thirty-five years earlier, had been anti-Islamic.[75]

By mid-1953, Kashani was urging the bazaars to support General Zahedi, the nominal leader of the prospective coup. He also praised the shah for being "young," "kindhearted," and highly "popular."[76] Kashani's closest supporters in Parliament, especially Shams Qanatabadi, Mozaffar Baqai, and Hosayn Makki (Modarres's biographer), denounced Mosaddeq as a dictator worse than Hitler and a Socialist more extreme than Stalin.[77] They also accused Mosaddeq of being anti-Islamic on the grounds that he endangered private property.[78] Hojjat al-Islam Mohammad Falsafi, a preacher who later became prominent in the Islamic Republic, actively participated in the coup by telling street audiences that Mosaddeq was intentionally paving the way for communism. The Fedayan-e Islam announced that they would cleanse Iran of such undesirable elements as Mosaddeq.

On the shah's triumphant return home on August 22, the Fedayan-e Islam newspaper hailed the coup as a "holy uprising," demanding Mosaddeq's execution and praising the shah as the world's Muslim hero.[79] Not surprisingly, Navab Safavi, their leader, was promptly released from prison and permitted to go on a world tour.[80] Meanwhile, Kashani told a foreign correspondent that Mosaddeq had fallen because he had forgotten that the shah enjoyed extensive popular support.[81] A month later, he went even further and declared that Mosaddeq deserved to be executed because he had committed the ultimate offense: rebelling against the shah, "betraying" the country, and repeatedly violating the sacred law.[82] Presumably this was Kashani's way of continuing the "crusade against imperialism and the Pahlavis."

Years later, when the Islamic Republic had been established, Falsafi praised Ayatollah Kashani as the real crusader against imperialism and the genuine precursor of Imam Khomeini. He also denounced Mosaddeq as a rabid secularist out to uproot religion from Iran.[83] Similarly, Hasan Ayat—who began his political career in Baqai's entourage and ended life as the most vocal lay proponent of theocracy—argued that Mosaddeq, despite his image, was really an "agent" of Anglo-American imperialism.[84] The evidence, according to him, was "overwhelming." Mosaddeq was an aristocrat who had joined the Freemasons in his youth, studied in Europe, and held numerous cabinet posts in the 1920s, which would have been impossible, so Ayat claimed, without British intrigue.

For his part, Khomeini often praised Kashani but rarely mentioned Mosaddeq. On one occasion, Khomeini claimed that unscrupulous secularists had so tarnished Kashani's reputation—as they had done to Shaykh Nuri earlier—that after 1953 this "great anti-imperialist fighter" had been too embarrassed to leave home. "People in the streets," Khomeini recounted, "would dress dogs as Ayatollah Kashani. Even fellow clerics lacked the courtesy to stand up when he entered a room."[85] Khomeini ended this speech by stressing the need for a proper understanding of history to undo the damage done by the unscrupulous secularists. But nowhere in this speech nor at any other public occasion did Khomeini explain why he had been conspiculously absent from politics in the turbulent years of 1951–53. Was this due to Borujerdi's ban or because he disliked Mosaddeq's secularism as much as that of the Pahlavis? He took the secret to his mausoleum.

5

The Paranoid Style
in Iranian Politics

We are not, like Allende [and Mosaddeq],
liberals willing to be snuffed out by the CIA.
Hojjat al-Islam Ali Khamenei, Ettela^cat,
5 March 1981

Introduction

Political polemics in Iran are replete with such terms as *tuteah*
(plot), *jasouz* (spy), *khianat* (treason), *vabasteh* (dependent),
khatar-e kharejeh (foreign danger), *^cummal-e kharejeh* (foreign
hands), *nafouz-e biganeh* (alien influence), *asrar* (secrets), *naq-
sheh* (designs), *^carosak* (marionette), *sotun-e panjom* (fifth column), *nokaran-e este^cmar* (servants of imperialism), *posht-e pardeh* (behind the curtain), and *posht-e sahneh* (behind the scene).
This vocabulary treats Iranian politics as a puppet show in which
foreign powers control the marionettes—the local politicians—by
invisible strings. The message is that the intelligent observer
should ignore appearances and focus instead on the hidden links;
only then can one follow the plot, understand the hidden agendas,
and identify the true villains. Needless to say, the picture assumes
the puppets are devoid of all initiative; the puppeteers are not only
omnipresent but also omniscient and omnipotent; and the play-
wright, whoever he may be, works to a grand scheme, knowing
beforehand exactly where to start the story, how to develop it, and
when to end it. Moreover, the plot, like any children's panto-

mime, is entertaining but contains no ambiguities, portraying the characters in absolute, good or evil terms.

The conspiratorial interpretation of politics is not, of course, unique to Iran. In fact, the title of this essay is borrowed from Richard Hofstadter's classic "The Paranoid Style in American Politics."[1] Published nearly thirty years ago, that article described how throughout American history nativistic groups have claimed that Washington was being subverted by foreign conspirators—at times by Freemasons, at other times by Roman Catholics, at yet other times by Jews, and, in more recent times, by International Communists, such as General Eisenhower and Chief Justice Earl Warren. Similarly, fearful politicians in Britain have been known to conjure up a variety of fantastic conspiracies—all the way from the Luddite-Jacobin plot during the Napoleonic Wars, to the Zionist "manipulation" of the 1908 revolution in the Ottoman Empire, and, more recently, to the KGB's "control" of Prime Minister Harold Wilson.[2] Such paranoia not only sees plots everywhere but views them as the main force of history. "According to this style history *is* a conspiracy," writes Hofstadter, "set in motion by demonic forces of almost transcendent power."[3]

Although the paranoid style can be found in many parts of the world, it is much more prevalent in modern Iran than in most Western societies. In the West, fears of plots, both real and imaginary, emerge in times of acute insecurity—during wars, revolutions, or economic crises. In Iran, they have been pervasive throughout the last half century. In the West, they tend to be confined to fringe groups, causing more ridicule than concern in the mainstream. In Iran, however, the paranoid style permeates society, the mainstream as much as the fringe, and cuts through all sectors of the political spectrum—royalists, nationalists, Communists, and, of course, Khomeinists. What stirs ridicule in Iran is not the style itself but the rival reading of the grand "conspiracy." One man's particular interpretation becomes for others not ridiculous but a deliberately misleading misinterpretation.

This chapter has three interrelated aims: first, to trace the root causes of the paranoid style in Iran; second, to compare the forms the style takes among the main political streams—among royalists, nationalists, and, most important of all, Khomeinists; and third, to weigh its consequences for contemporary Iran, especially its costs in retarding the development of political pluralism.

Causes

Observers—from Victorian travelers to American social scientists—have argued that Iranian politics is marked by a high degree of paranoia as well as mistrust, insecurity, and factionalism. Lord Curzon concluded his encyclopedic *Persia and the Persian Question* with the comment that the "natives are a suspicious people" who tend to "see a cloven hoof beneath the skirt of every robe."[4] Professor Ann Lambton, in a much quoted work from the 1950s, remarked that "factionalism, in one form or another, has remained a feature of Persian life down to modern times."[5] Herbert Vreeland, in his introduction to the famous *Human Relations Area Files*, asserted that "insecurity and distrust permeate Persian attitudes toward each other . . . the individual has a psychological wall out of which he reaches to play his game of life."[6] Andrew Westwood, in explaining why the monarchy survived the turbulent 1950s, claimed that the "culture of distrust" not only fragmented the opposition but also predisposed the public to view politicians as "corrupt," "mendacious," and "foreign-connected."[7] Similarly, Hooshang Amirahmadi, in discussing the Islamic Republic's economic failures, places responsibility on the country's "obsolete political culture," which

> is characterized by ideological dogmatism, political extremism, chauvinistic heroism, vulnerability to personality cult, subservience and fear of authority, cynicism, distrust, disunity, and individualism. . . . The paranoia associated with this conspiratorial view of politics is largely cross-class and cross-ideological. It is, however, widespread among Iranian political elites and intelligentsia who continue to use it as a weapon against political enemies or for manipulation of the followers.[8]

Most observers trace these "maladies" to "national culture" in general and to child-rearing practices in particular. In Vreeland's view, for instance, the "Persian learns his basic attitude towards authority in the family."[9] The shah, in arguing in favor of strong government, continually harped on the presumed "weak moral fiber of the Iranians."[10] Marvin Zonis, the author of the main quantitative study on the Pahlavi elite, appears to conclude that their peculiar child-raising customs result in adults who, in his own words, are paranoid, insecure, cynical, distrustful, disdainful, dishonest, pessimistic, subservient, manipulative, xenophobic, opportunistic, timid, individualistic, egoistical, and megalomanic.[11]

Western diplomats, especially when frustrated by Iranian politics, readily resorted to such "national character" explanations. For example, the British consul in Isfahan, upon failing to create an anti-Communist labor movement during World War II, complained that "no two Persians can ever work together for any length of time, even if it is jointly to extract money from a third party."[12] Similarly, one British ambassador, fearful of Soviet influence in the aftermath of the battle of Stalingrad, wrote of a "volatile race" without "principles."[13] "Only the prospect of making an illicit fortune seems to give the Persian, including the young, courage and energy."[14] He also warned: "It is regrettable, but a fact, that the Persians are ideal Stalin-fodder. They are untruthful, backbiters, undisciplined, incapable of unity, without a plan. The Soviet system is equipped with a complete theoretical scheme for everything from God to galoshes."[15] Another British ambassador declared that these "failings" were not passing phases but the "permanent weaknesses" of the "Oriental character."[16] Similarly, the U.S. ambassador, showing off his classical education, warned Washington: "In our dealings with the Medes and Persians we must always recall that we have to do with a people for whom advantages of the day suffice. They are not without talent and ability, but they disdain the past and ignore the future."[17]

These imperial, even racist, attitudes are encapsulated in a 1951 Foreign Office memorandum drafted to explain why Iranians were so "emotional" as to reject the "reasonable" argument that their oil industry should continue to remain under British control for an indefinite period of time. Entitled "Paper on the Persian Social and Political Scene," the memorandum explained:

> Most Persians are introverts. Their imagination is strong and they naturally turn to the agreeable side of things. They love poetry and discussion, particularly of abstract ideas. . . . Their emotions are strong and easily aroused. But they continually fail to subordinate their emotions to reason. They lack commonsense and the ability to examine and reason from facts. Their well-known mendacity is rather a carelessness of the truth than a deliberate choice of false-hood. This excess of imagination and distaste for facts leads to an inability to go conscientiously into detail. Often, after finding the world does not answer their dreams, they relapse into indolence and do not persevere in any attempt to bring their ideas into focus with reality. This tendency is exaggerated by the fatalism of their religion. They are intensely individualistic, more in the sense of pursuing their personal interests than in the nobler one of wishing to do things on their own without help. Nearly all classes have a passion for personal gain. . . . They lack social conscience and are unready to submit to communal interests. They are vain, conceited, and unwilling to admit themselves in any wrong.[18]

These explanations have obvious flaws. They reduce complex phenomena to one residual category—to that ever-elusive category known as "national character."[19] They are highly ahistorical, often based on Jungian assumptions, accepting national character as an unchanging entity rooted in some unstated source—maybe in "race," "ethnicity," or "folk mythology." They jump from impressionistic observations of a few people, invariably members of the elite, to blanket generalizations about the whole population, one that is in reality extremely diverse. They provide little information about child-rearing but, again because of their psychological assumptions, presume that the "maladies" can be traced to child-parent relationships. What is more, they lump together a variety of maladies, assuming them to be present in equal proportions among most Iranians.

Nevertheless, most observers would agree that political paranoia exists in modern Iran, as long as one keeps in mind Hofstadter's important caveat that the term means merely a political style and mode of expression, not a clinical and deep-seated psychological disorder. What is more, this style can be explained by history, especially Iran's experience of imperial domination: foreign powers—first Russia and Britain, later the United States—have, in fact, determined the principal formations in the country's political landscape over the last two hundred years.

These key formations include three disastrous wars in the first half of the nineteenth century; the subsequent capitulations in the treaties of Golestan, Turkmanchai, and Paris; the creation of the Tsarist-led Cossack Brigade in 1879; the sale of the tobacco monopoly to a British entrepreneur in 1890; the 1901 D'Arcy concession, which soon led to the establishment of the Anglo-Persian Oil Company; the 1907 Anglo-Russian Agreement, dividing Iran into zones of influence; the 1911 Russian Ultimatum and the consequent Anglo-Russian occupation; and the 1919 Anglo-Persian Agreement, designed to make the whole country into a British protectorate. In the eyes of not only Iranians but also other Europeans, Russia and Britain had in effect incorporated Iran into their empires. It was their diplomats who ruled the country; the shah served as a "mere viceroy."[20] By the second half of the century, the Qajar shahs could not even designate their successors without the explicit approval of the two imperial representatives.

Imperial influence was also present in Iran's three military coups: in 1908, 1921, and 1953. In the first, the Cossack Brigade led by its Tsarist officers bombarded the newly established Parliament in an attempt to shore up the faltering Qajar monarchy. In the second, British officers helped Colonel Reza Khan of the same Cossack Brigade to overthrow the government, paving the way for the demise of the Qajar dynasty and the birth of the Pahlavi state. In the third, the CIA, together with Britain's MI6, financed army officers to overthrow a popular prime minister and salvage the Pahlavi throne. These traumatic events naturally led Iranians to conclude that whatever took place in their country was decided by the imperial powers.

This feeling of alienation was further intensified by the wide gap existing between state and civil society—in Persian terms, between the *dawlat* (government) and *mellat* (nation); the *mamlekat* (realm) and *ummat* (community); the *darbar* (court) and *vatan* (country); the *hokumat* (regime) and *mardom* (people).

The imperial powers sought local clients, and the elite in turn sought foreign patrons, even foreign citizenship. Ordinary citizens, thus, understandably came to the conclusion that public figures harbored alien "ties" and "connections." In the words of a typical Iranian historian: "The imperial powers interfered in everything, even the personal affairs of leading statesmen. Absolutely nothing could be done without their permission."[21]

The link between the imperial powers and local elites was most glaring from 1941 to 1953—from Reza Shah's abdication brought about by the Anglo-Soviet invasion to Mohammad Reza Shah's triumphant return engineered by the CIA. For one thing, this period saw the birth of Iran's main political movements, especially the Tudeh and the National Front, and a host of gadfly newspapers which were able to openly air such themes as class conflict, national sovereignty, and foreign intervention. For another, the Great Powers immersed themselves in Iranian politics while Iranian politicians actively sought their help.

The shah, convinced that the army and the monarchy would stand or fall together, sought U.S. military aid. Southern politicians—led by Sayyid Ziya, a leading figure in the 1921 coup—obtained British assistance to counter both the shah and their other competitors. The United States considered Sayyid Ziya to be so pro-British as to be "unsuitable" for the premiership.[22] Americans, no less than Iranians, were highly skeptical when British officials, such as Lambton, categorically denied having ties with Sayyid Ziya.[23] Northern aristocrats tried to contain the shah and their southern rivals first by seeking Soviet help, but when they found the Soviets encouraging social revolution in Iran, they turned to the United States, seeking economic, rather than military, assistance. The Tudeh party, on the other hand, as a radical movement, looked to the Soviet Union as the "champion of the international working class." Meanwhile, Mosaddeq, leading the middle-class National Front, sought U.S. support against the pro-British aristocrats associated with the Anglo-Iranian Oil Company, against the shah and the armed forces, against the pro-Soviet Tudeh, and against the northern aristocrats as well as conservative pro-American politicians.

Riding a wave of popularity based on his promise to nationalize oil, Mosaddeq was elected premier in 1951 and promptly took over the Anglo-Iranian Oil Company. The British, refusing to accept nationalization, did their best to discredit Mosaddeq, categorizing him as a "wily Oriental" who was not only "crazy," "eccentric," "abnormal," "unbalanced," and "unreasonable" but also "demagogic," "slippery," "cunning," "unscrupulous," "single-mindedly obstinate," and "opium-addicted."[24] "Mosaddeq's megalomania," declared the British Embassy in 1952, "is now verging on mental instability. He has to be humoured like a fractious child."[25] As evidence of Mosaddeq's "mental instability," the British ambassador cited his refusal to use the ministerial motorcar and the title "His Excellency."[26] He concluded that Iran, unlike the rest of Asia, was not yet ready for independence but rather, like Haiti, needed some twenty more years of foreign occupation: "Persia is indeed rather like a man who knows very well that he ought to go to the dentist but is afraid of doing so and is annoyed with anybody who says there is anything wrong with his teeth."[27]

The British government planted articles with similar themes in the newspapers. For example, the *London Times* carried a biography of Mosaddeq describing him as "nervously unstable," "martyr-like," and "timid" unless "emotionally" aroused.[28] The *Observer* depicted him as an "incorruptible fanatic," a xenophobic Robespierre, a "tragic" Frankenstein "impervious to common sense," and with only "one political idea in his gigantic head."[29] To encourage similar views across the Atlantic, the British fed the American press with a steady diet of—to use their own words— "poison too venomous for the BBC."[30] Typical of such character assassinations was an article in the *Washington Post* written by the venerable Drew Pearson falsely accusing Hosayn Fatemi, Mosaddeq's right-hand man, of a host of criminal offenses, including embezzlement and gangsterism. "This man," Pearson warned, "will eventually decide whether the US has gas rationing, or possibly, whether the American people go into World War III."[31]

The British, determined to undermine Mosaddeq from the day he was elected premier, refused to negotiate seriously with him.

For instance, Professor Lambton, serving as a Foreign Office consultant, advised as early as November 1951 that the British government should persevere in "undermining" Mosaddeq, refuse to reach agreement with him, and reject American attempts to find a compromise solution. "The Americans," she insisted, "do not have the experience or the psychological insight to understand Persia."[32]

The central figure in the British strategy to overthrow Mosaddeq was another academic, Robin Zaehner, who soon became professor of Eastern religions and ethics at Oxford. As press attaché in Tehran during 1943–47, Zaehner had befriended numerous politicians, especially through opium-smoking parties. Dispatched back to Iran by MI6, Zaehner actively searched for a suitable general to carry out the planned coup.[33] He also used diverse channels to undermine Mosaddeq: Sayyid Ziya and the pro-British politicians; newspaper editors up for sale; conservative aristocrats who in the past had sided with Russia and America; tribal chiefs, notably the Bakhtiyaris; army officers, shady businessmen, courtiers, and members of the royal family, many of whom outstripped the shah in their fear of Mosaddeq. Helped in due course by the CIA, Zaehner also wooed away a number of Mosaddeq's associates, including Ayatollah Kashani, General Zahedi, Hosayn Makki, and Mozaffar Baqai.[34] Baqai, a professor of ethics at Tehran University, soon became notorious as the man who abducted Mosaddeq's chief of police and tortured him to death. MI6, together with the CIA, also resorted to dirty tricks to undermine the government, one of the more harmless ones being the rumor that "the communists are plotting against Mosaddeq's life and placing the responsibility on the British."[35]

It is therefore not surprising that the 1953 coup gave rise to conspiracy theories, including cloak and dagger stories of Orientalist professors moonlighting as spies, forgers, and even assassins. Reality—in this case—was stranger than fiction. These conspiracy theories were compounded by the fact that some Western academics did their best to expurgate from their publications any mention of the CIA and MI6 in the 1953 coup. In fact, recent autobiographies reveal that the shah often subsidized British and

American academics whose publications tended to reinforce the court view of modern Iranian history, especially of the 1953 events.[36]

Expressions

The paranoid style permeates Iranian politics, but the various political groups vary the plot and cast of characters. For Khomeinists, *este^Cmar* (colonialism-imperialism), helped by the *sotun-e panjom* (fifth column), formed of diverse minorities, is a constant threat to the Muslim people of Iran. For the Left, imperialists are plotting with the upper class against the country's workers and peasants. For the National Front, imperialism, but this time more as a political phenomenon, has gained a stranglehold over Iran by overthrowing Mosaddeq, the nation's only genuine spokesman. For the royalists, the foreign powers, particularly Britain and Russia, have consistently conspired to destroy the Pahlavi dynasty in general and Mohammad Reza Shah in particular.

In Khomeini's works "colonial conspiracies" lurked everywhere. He blamed them for the age-old problems of the Middle East: the decline of Muslim civilization, the conservative "distortions" of Islam, and the divisions between nation-states, between Sunnis and Shiis, and between oppressors and oppressed.[37] He argued that the colonial powers had for years sent Orientalists into the East to misinterpret Islam and the Koran[38] and that the colonial powers had conspired to undermine Islam both with religious quietism and with secular ideologies, especially socialism, liberalism, monarchism, and nationalism *(mellitgarayi)*.[39] He claimed that Britain had instigated the 1905 Constitutional Revolution to subvert Islam: "The Iranians who drafted the constitutional laws were receiving instructions directly from their British masters."[40]

Khomeini also held the West responsible for a host of contemporary problems. He charged that colonial conspiracies kept the country poor and backward, exploited its resources, inflamed class antagonisms, divided the clergy and alienated them from the masses, caused mischief among the tribes, infiltrated the universi-

Figure 14. Cartoon from the satirical leftist journal *Ahanger* (16 April 1979) depicting Iran in a chess match with the United States. Iran's chess pieces are workers, peasants, students, the Fedayin, and the Mojahedin. The U.S. chess pieces are the CIA, military advisers, prison torturers, and "liberals" such as Banisadr, Qotbzadeh, and Dr. Yazdi.

Figure 15. Cartoon from *Ahanger* (8 May 1979). The United States startles Iran by moving Yazdi, the minister of foreign affairs. The "liberals" are seen as mere pieces controlled by the foreign hand.

ties, cultivated consumer instincts, and encouraged moral corruption, especially gambling, prostitution, drug addiction, and alcohol consumption.[41] He claimed that the West spread cultural imperialism and false notions of Islam through its control of schools, universities, publishing houses, journals, newspapers, and radio and television.[42] "Colonialism," he declared, "has poisoned the minds of our youth. It is determined to keep them weak."[43] At times he argued that the West harnessed the Eastern Bloc against Islam.[44]

During the Islamic Revolution, Khomeini found "plots," here, there, and everywhere. "The world," he proclaimed, "is against us."[45] He even used the terms Left and Right to describe how the newly established republic was supposedly besieged by royalists as well as Marxists.[46] "Satanic plots" lurked behind liberal Muslims favoring a lay, rather than a clerical, constitution; behind conservative Muslims opposed to his interpretation of *velayat-e faqih;* behind apolitical Muslims who preferred the seminaries to the hustle-and-bustle of politics; behind radical Muslims advocating root-and-branch social changes; behind lawyers critical of the harsh retribution laws; behind Kurds, Arabs, Baluchis, and Turkomans seeking regional autonomy; behind leftists organizing strikes and trade unions; and, of course, behind military officers sympathetic to the Pahlavis, the National Front, and even President Banisadr.[47] He labeled the pro-Soviet Left as "Russian spies," the anti-Soviet Left as "American Marxists," and the conservative Muslims as "American Muslims."

He considered the Mojahedin the most dangerous of these fifth columnists. Playing on words, he likened the Mojahedin to the notorious *monafeqin* (hypocrites), who in the Koran had pretended to support the Prophet while secretly conspiring against him with Jews and pagans. "In the name of Islam," he warned, "the *monafeqin* want to destroy Islam."[48] He also likened the Mojahedin to a recently converted Jew at the time of Imam Ali who incessantly cited the Koran without understanding its true meaning.[49] "The country," he stressed, "is threatened by a conspiracy involving the *monafeqin*, the Left, the liberals, and the nationalists."[50]

Khomeini also warned that the West, in its desire to dominate the world, had an insatiable desire to collect information on Iran:

> The Big Powers, and among them especially the United States, have since long ago been busy scheming. And preceding them was Britain. For a long time now they have been putting together the sporadic bits of information and intelligence which they have gathered about the various countries of the world and specifically those upon which they have preyed. What we have in terms of natural resources, they know better than we do. Even before the advent of motorcars they would dispatch their experts here to make a survey of our resources on horseback or camel and along with caravans in order to survey our mineral resources, including our oil as well as our valuable stones. I recall I mentioned in an earlier speech my meeting with a member of the Qom Theological School during my trip to Hamedan many years ago. He was the son of a well-reputed personality in the city of Hamedan and he brought me this map which was strewn with small dots. I asked him what the dots represented, and he told me the map had been drawn by agents of a foreign power and the dots represented the presence of mineral resources in that region of the country. It was a fully detailed map showing even the smallest villages. Therefore, as you can see, even at a time when automobiles were not in vogue, they had surveyed the whole of our country including our deserts on camels and had at the same time studied the ethnic life of the people here, as well as their social life, their habits, their religion, their tastes, their inclinations, and also learned about the clerics here, as well as about the relations between the *ulama* and the masses and so on and so forth.[51]

Khomeini assigned a particularly sinister role to the religious minorities, especially the Jews, to whom he often referred with the derogatory term *yahodi* rather than the more neutral *kalimi*. He accused them of distorting Islam, mistranslating the Koran, persecuting and imprisoning the clergy, advocating historical materialism, instigating the so-called White Revolution, applauding the 1963 bloodshed, controlling the mass media, and, of course, taking over the economy.[52] The Jews were depicted as imperialist spies, agents, and fifth columnists. They were seen as the real power behind the imperialists plotting to take over the whole world: "Their true aim is to establish a world Jewish government.''[53] Khomeini added that there was a danger they would achieve this aim since Jews were "energetic and very shrewd [*zalum*]." Khomeini also denounced the Bahais as a "subversive conspiracy" and a "secret political organization" that had originally been created by Britain but now was controlled by Israel and the United States. "Reagan supports the Bahais," he argued, "in the same way the Soviets control the Tudeh. The Bahais are not a religion but a secretive organization plotting to subvert the Islamic Republic.''[54]

Khomeini's supporters were equally paranoid. A prominent cleric issued a proclamation reminding the faithful that chapter 5, verse 56, of the Koran warned them not to befriend Jews and Christians.[55] Ruhani, Khomeini's main hagiographer, asserted that SAVAK (the secret police) had instructions to kill those who dared to criticize Jewish capitalists "such as Nelson Rockefeller.''[56] Hojjat al-Islam Sa'edi, a cleric tortured to death in 1970 in prison, preached that Jews "like Lyndon Johnson" controlled America. He also preached that the Bahais had taken over the Iranian economy, and the shah was working hand-in-glove with Bahais and Communists against true Muslims.[57] Khamenei claimed, in the same breath, that East and West conspired together against Iran and that at the same time they competed with each other for Tehran's favor.[58] *Kayhan-e Hava'i* argued that the Bahais had always worked as foreign slaves *(ghulam)*, first for the Tsarists, then for the British and Ottomans, and now for the Israelis and Americans.[59] *Ettela^Cat* linked Kasravi, the secular historian, to Reza Shah, and the latter to the international imperialist plot.[60] The same paper argued that secular nationalism was a bourgeois ideology created by imperialism to sow dissension in the Muslim world and divide the people from the clergy.[61] Similarly, history textbooks describe Bahaism as a "political conspiracy" hatched by nineteenth-century European imperialists to break the unity of Islam.[62]

Khomeinists did not confine their search for conspiracies to Iranian politics. A public meeting organized by the regime in 1990 claimed that Marxism was a Jewish plot and that Salman Rushdie's *Satanic Verses* was part of the Israeli conspiracy to destroy

Islam.[63] In a long series of articles on imperialism, *Kayhan-e Hava'i* argued that some historians felt the past was shaped by "great men," others by the "common man," but in reality the true force behind events had been conspirators—especially Freemasons, Jews, or the two combined.[64] Such conspiracies had brought about the Stuart Restoration in England, the partitioning of Poland and the Ottoman Empire, and, of course, the American, French, and Russian revolutions. The Bolshevik Revolution, the articles asserted, was an integral element in the Jewish conspiracy to take over the whole world. As evidence, the articles referred to the "Protocols of the Elders of Zion," the flow of "Jewish gold" into the Russian underground, and the ethnic origins of Marx, Trotsky, Kamenev, and Zinoviev. Even Stalin was named part of this conspiracy on the grounds that his wife was Jewish. These Jews were responsible for the persecution of the Muslim peoples of central Asia. These conspiracy theories would have won the approval of Louis XIV, not to mention Tsar Nicholas II. These paranoid fantasies should not be dismissed as the ranting and raving of the lunatic fringe; *Kayhan-e Hava'i* is a "highbrow paper" written for graduates studying in Western universities, that is, the crème de la crème of the Islamic Republic.

The paranoid style of the National Front comes out clearly in a book entitled *Nabard-e Pruzheh-ha-ye Siyasi dar Sahneh-e Iran* (The struggles of political projects in the Iranian scene).[65] Its author, Hosayn Malek, was a veteran Mosaddeqist, who, together with his elder brother Khalel Maleki, had created the "social democratic" wing of the National Front. The two had joined the Tudeh in the early 1940s but had left it in 1946 to form an independent Marxist organization. Active in the 1979 revolution, Hosayn Malek was forced to flee Iran in 1981 when Khomeini cracked down on the opposition, including the National Front. He wrote this book in Europe a few years before his death (from natural causes).

The book, which is replete with charts and diagrams, argues that the imperialists have incessantly schemed to subvert Iran. Every political organization—of course, with the notable exception of the National Front—is categorized as part of this or that foreign scheme. The Russians worked not only through the Tudeh, the Fedayin, and the Mojahedin but also through—believe it or not—Khomeini's inner circle. "Behind these clerics," Malek claims, "lurk the Soviets." The British conspired through the Bahais, Freemasons, Fedayan-e Islam, and most especially senior clerics. The British could work with the clergy because Islam was an "Arab ideology" and everyone knew that the English histori- cally controlled the Arab world. Even Jamal al-Din Afghani, the famous nineteenth-century pan-Islamist, was seen as part of this British plot.[66]

Malek went on to argue that the Americans channeled their activities through the Pahlavis, the military, the large corpora- tions, the Freemasons, the liberal parties (notably Bazargan's Lib- eration Movement), and defectors from the National Front. In fact, according to Malek, Mosaddeq had been the victim of a highly complicated plot involving not only the CIA, MI6, the royal- ist generals, the clerical leaders, and the Fedayan-e Islam but also the Tudeh, which he linked to Britain as well as Russia. The Tudeh, in turn, took the position that the oil nationalization crisis was a struggle between America and Britain and that the National Front was merely a "U.S. instrument" forged to supplant one imperialism with another.[67]

The notion that the Tudeh worked for the British, however farfetched, has a long pedigree within the National Front.[68] Mosaddeq himself had dubbed the Tudeh as "oil communists." These charges were based on the following "facts." During World War II, the Tudeh had joined a group of pro-British editors in creating a newspaper alliance known as the Anti-Fascist Society. Lambton, as the wartime British press attaché, had had frequent dealings with prominent intellectuals, many of whom happened to be left-leaning. The Tudeh had initially been ambivalent about Mosaddeq's nationalization campaign, instead calling for conces- sions to the Soviets in the north and the prompt expropriation without compensation of the British company in the south. The final clincher was the "discovery" in the Abadan offices of the Anglo-Iranian Oil Company of "secret documents" proving that the British were supporting the Tudeh. In actual fact, these documents were forgeries planted by Baqai supporters. The forgeries were so crude that they did not even bother to use the company's paper, numbering codes, and transliteration system.[69]

British officials not only lacked links with the Tudeh but, together with their American counterparts, complained that they found it impossible to penetrate the wall of secrecy surrounding that party's leadership.[70] The U.S. State Department was so ignorant of the inner workings of the Tudeh that its main handbook on communism in Iran, written in 1950, argued the party's real leaders were not the acknowledged ones but veteran Bolsheviks hiding in Russia.[71] In fact, the veteran Bolsheviks named here had been killed by Stalin some twenty years earlier—so much for the notion that the imperial powers were all-knowing.

The reader may be tempted to dismiss these conspiratorial notions as leftist, nationalist, and Khomeinist paranoia. The style, however, was no less prevalent among royalists, whom the American media generally referred to as "moderate," "realistic," and "down-to-earth." The shah's last memoir, *Answer to History*, reads like a long nightmare full of shadowy figures out to knife him. According to him, the British, because they liked to "meddle in everything," had "a hand" in the creation of the Tudeh party.[72] The attempt on his life in 1949 had been plotted jointly by the Tudeh, the "ultraconservative" clergy, and the British, who liked to have "their fingers in strange pies" and whose embassy gardener was the father of the mistress of the would-be assassin.[73] Mosaddeq, despite his "public posturing," was really a British agent who had agreed to take the premiership during World War II on condition he received his "master's explicit approval."[74] Shahpour Bakhtiyar, premier on the eve of the revolution, was also an agent of British Petroleum.[75] The Tudeh had infiltrated the National Front, elevated Khomeini to the rank of ayatollah, and created "an unholy" alliance with the Right to instigate both the 1963 bloodshed and the 1979 revolution.[76] The oil companies had also played an important role in the revolution for they had never forgiven him for making a highly favorable deal with an Italian entrepreneur, whom they had murdered.[77] The CIA, for unstated reasons, had for years financed the clergy.[78]

The shah's paranoia reaches its peak when discussing the 1979 revolution. He claims that his overthrow was brought about by a "strange amalgam" of not only the clergy, the Tudeh, and the oil companies but also the Western media and, of course, the Carter and Thatcher administrations.[79] The joke going around royalist circles after the revolution was if you lifted Khomeini's beard you would find inscribed "Made in Britain."

The religious minorities are conspicuous in their absence from the shah's memoirs. This, however, does not mean that they did not figure in royalist paranoia. In 1957 the regime, probably with CIA help, published with much fanfare a propaganda book against the Tudeh implying that the Soviets found the Christian community in Iran fertile ground for recruiting spies and subversives.[80] The shah himself, in a private conversation with an American human rights lawyer on the eve of the revolution, argued that the Western press was Jewish controlled and that was why it had taken him to task over SAVAK as soon as he had begun to side with the Palestinians.[81] This would have been news to the Israelis, not to mention the Palestinians. Similarly, a royalist pamphlet published in 1979 argued that Khomeini, "who cannot even speak Persian properly," had been installed in power by a formidable international conspiracy. This conspiracy included not only the oil companies, the Communists, and the superpowers but also Freemasons, Western companies who did not want Iran to industrialize, and Zionists, who "control 70 percent of the world's investments in giant industries."[82]

The shah's private conversations with his adviser and longtime friend Asadollah Alam are also highly revealing.[83] He was convinced that Britain worked through the Tudeh, the senior clergy, including Khomeini, and the Baathist regime in Iraq. He was equally convinced that the Soviets were behind student disturbances in Iran, and the oil companies were instigating the Marxist as well as the Muslim guerrilla organizations against his regime. He even suspected that a "hidden force" controlled the United States, assassinating Kennedy and anyone else who got wind of its existence. If he had lived long enough, Mohammad Reza Shah Pahlavi could have found employment in Hollywood as a consultant to the film *JFK*.

Royalist paranoia appears clearly in the 1988 television "confession" of General Hosayn Fardoust, the shah's childhood friend who for years headed the Imperial Inspectorate, a security agency second only to SAVAK.[84] Even though this confession, like all television confessions, should be taken with a grain of salt, it does reflect the royalist mentality—at least, features of that mentality which the new regime considered plausible for the general public. Besides dwelling on Mohammad Reza Shah's amorous adventures, Fardoust "revealed" the inner affairs of the royal palace. He claimed that Reza Shah had been a secret Bahai; Foroughi, the wartime premier, was a Freemason and therefore a British agent; and the royal palace was so full of British spies that even the shah could not speak freely there. Fardoust also claimed that over 30 percent of the leaders of the National Front were secret Tudehis; the British secretly favored Mosaddeq and his campaign to nationalize the oil company; the National Front was "linked" to the United States; the British arranged the young shah's marriage to and divorce from Princess Fawzieh of Egypt; Queen Elizabeth had personally ordered the shah to set up the Imperial Inspectorate; and Ernest Perron, another of the shah's childhood friends, had been placed by the British in Le Rosey School in Switzerland to establish ties with the future shah. Fardoust also claimed that MI6 rather than the CIA had saved the throne in 1953 and that the latter, left on its own, would have installed a military dictatorship.

Fardoust died a few weeks after the publication of these confessions. Three years later, *Kayhan-e Hava'i* serialized, in both Persian and English, what were purported to be Fardoust's more detailed memoirs.[85] These claimed that Perron had been planted by the British in Le Rosey to seduce the young shah; that Perron headed a homosexual clique among the courtiers and the Freemasons; and that he continued to work for MI6 until his death in 1961, when his espionage role was taken over by Dr. Ayadi, a Bahai veterinary surgeon who had cured the shah of a psychosomatic ailment. Ayadi was described as the Rasputin of Iran. These memoirs also elaborated on the theme that Mosaddeq was a British agent. They argued that Mosaddeq could not have attained high positions in the 1920s without London's support and that his close friend Alam was a "well-known" British agent. To top it all, the memoirs claimed that Mosaddeq, because of these foreign ties, had consciously helped the MI6 and CIA carry out the coup against himself.

Consequences

Given the imperial experience, some of the suspicions of foreign conspiracies were quite plausible. The British did want Mosaddeq's removal, did have contacts with senior clerics, did seek information about the Tudeh, and at times did have policy differences with the shah. Similarly, the Russians and the Americans actively sought contacts, influence, information, and, thereby, operatives. After all, the KGB, CIA, and MI6 are not mere figments of a fertile imagination. Even paranoids can have enemies. But accepting this does not mean that the main actors on the Iranian scene, whether politicians or political parties, were mere marionettes controlled by the Great Powers. The paranoid style distorted the overall picture, not just the details.

The paranoid style had far-reaching consequences. The premise that grand plots existed naturally led to the belief there were plotters everywhere—some obvious, others more devious. And if one were surrounded by plotters, one could conclude that those with views different from one's own were members of this or that foreign conspiracy. Thus political activists tended to equate competition with treason, liberalism with weak-mindedness, honest differences of opinion with divisive alien conspiracies, and political toleration with permissiveness toward the enemy within.

The result was detrimental for the development of political pluralism in Iran. Political coalitions were difficult to launch, and when in the rare cases they were launched, they could quickly be shipwrecked on the treacherous rocks of mutual distrust and widespread suspicion. Differences of opinion within organizations could not be accommodated; it was all too easy for leaders to expel dissidents as "foreign agents." Moreover, the rulers—Khomeini as much as the shah—could readily exploit public paranoia, associating the opposition with this or that foreign conspiracy. Furthermore, the regimes, in eliminating the opposition, could easily charge them with the ultimate political crime: that of treason, espionage, and foreign subversion. One does not compromise and negotiate with spies and traitors; one locks them up or else shoots them.

The paranoid style, thus, paved the way for the mass executions of 1981–82. When in June 1981 the Mojahedin tried to overthrow the Islamic Republic, Khomeini proclaimed that the CIA was planning a repeat performance of 1953 and that the whole opposition, not just the Mojahedin, was implicated in this grand "international plot." In six short weeks, the Islamic Republic shot over one thousand prisoners. The victims included not only members of the Mojahedin but also royalists, Bahais, Jews, Kurds, Baluchis, Arabs, Qashqayis, Turkomans, National Frontists, Maoists, anti-Stalinist Marxists, and even apolitical teenage girls who happened to be in the wrong street at the wrong time. Never before in Iran had firing squads executed so many in so short a time over so flimsy an accusation. Real fears had merged with unreal ones. The paranoid style had produced tragedy as well as comedy.

Epilogue

Ever since the revolution, our foreign enemies
and their domestic agents have conspired to
distort the imam's true message—especially
the message that Islam's main concern is the
oppressed. They now have the audacity to
declare that the age of Imam Khomeini is
over, the age of combating capitalist leeches
is over, the age of danger from the world-
devouring America is over.

> A. Bayat, parliamentary speech, Resalat,
> 1 March 1990

Some pseudoclerics don't realize that to obey
God we must obey the Prophet; to obey the
Prophet we must obey Imam Ali; to obey
Imam Ali we must obey the clergy, especially
Imam Khomeini; and to obey Imam Khomeini
we must obey his successor, His Eminence
Ayatollah Khamenei, the leader of the Islamic
Revolution. . . . These pseudoclerics don't
realize that on questions of government, one
cannot emulate a deceased man. One must
emulate the living leader.

> Ayatollah Azari-Qomi, Friday sermon, Resalat,
> 24 February 1990

Khomeini, like populists the world over, modified his rhetoric
depending on political circumstances. In 1979–82, at the height of
the revolution, he equated Islam with social justice, especially fair

income distribution. He praised the oppressed, the barefooted, and the shantytown poor, and denounced the oppressors, the rich, the greedy palace dwellers, and their foreign patrons. But after 1982, as Iran's Thermidor began, he equated Islam with respect for private property, described the bazaar as an essential pillar of society, and emphasized the importance of government as well as law and order. Khomeini viewed this not as a shift of position but as a change of emphasis within the parameters of his broad-based movement. In the 1979–82 period, he had used radical rhetoric to mobilize the urban populace against the Pahlavi monarchy. But in the 1982–89 period, he toned down his language to institutionalize the revolution and build the Islamic Republic, which increasingly took the shape of a propertied middle-class republic.

Most of Khomeini's disciples can be divided into two groups, though all declare themselves to be faithful and militant followers of the *khatt-e imam* (imam's line).[1] At one end are the militant populists, who can be labeled radicals for want of a better term. They are often referred to as the *tund-ru* (fast walkers), *faqih-e motarraqi* (progressive jurists), and *faqih-e mostazafin* (pro-poor jurists). Most are members of the Majm^C-e Ruhaniyn-e Mobarez (Society of the Militant Clergy). At the other end are those who can be called moderates: they are referred to as *mianeh-ru* (middle roaders) and *faqih-e sunnati* (traditional jurists). They are organized into the Jam^{C}eh-e Ruhaniat-e Mobarez (Association of the Militant Clergy).

The radicals sometimes denounce the moderates as rightists, pro-American Muslims, and *faqih-e sarmayehdari* (capitalist jurists). The moderates, in turn, denounce the radicals as etatists, extreme leftists, and pro-Soviet Muslims. Khomeini himself constantly shifted the weight of his support from one group to the other, making sure that neither gained ascendancy. He knew perfectly well that if the radicals gained control they would antagonize the bazaar, the pillar of the Islamic Republic. He also knew that if the moderates obtained complete power they would alienate the shantytown poor, the revolution's main battering ram. Khomeini thus slowed down the drift toward the Thermidor.

The Thermidor quickened within weeks of Khomeini's death in

June 1989. Power passed quickly to a diumvirate formed of Hojjat al-Islam Khamenei and Hojjat al-Islam Rafsanjani. The Assembly of Experts promptly hailed Khamenei as an ayatollah and named him to be the imam's successor as the Supreme Faqih and Rahbar (Leader) of the Islamic Republic. The regime admitted that Khamenei lacked the scholarly qualifications of many other senior clerics but pronounced him more suited for the exalted position on the grounds that he was highly knowledgeable of the "contemporary problems facing the Muslim world." The head of the Assembly of Experts declared that Khamenei had been chosen because he had been close to the imam, had played important roles in both the revolution and the war with Iraq, and was familiar with the social, political, and economic issues facing Muslims.[2] Rafsanjani claimed that on his deathbed the imam had expressed his wish that Khamenei should succeed him as Leader.[3]

Rafsanjani, hitherto the Speaker of Parliament and the acting commander in chief of the armed forces, replaced Khamenei as president. Meanwhile, the power of the presidency was greatly increased through constitutional amendments that abolished the post of prime minister and handed much of his authority to the president. Khamenei and Rafsanjani assured the public that they would faithfully follow the road laid out by Imam Khomeini. To keep future debate within bounds, Parliament passed a bill making it illegal for anyone to misuse, misquote, or misinterpret the works of the imam.

Despite their assurances, Rafsanjani and Khamenei spent the next three years squeezing the radicals out of influential positions. A portent of the future appeared in November 1989, when Rafsanjani presented a long eulogy in which he played down Khomeini's role as the charismatic leader of the downtrodden masses.[4] Rafsanjani depicted him instead as a first-rank theologian and philosopher, especially on mysticism, as a major scholar who had given "a new lease on life" to the Qom seminaries, and as a world-famous figure who had restored Iran's national sovereignty. He even praised him as an innovative senior cleric who had performed the "miracle" of bringing Islam out of the "graveyard." The word *mostazafin* was hardly mentioned.

Rafsanjani and Khamenei were helped in their campaign against the radicals by the powerful Council of Guardians, which had been the bastion of the conservative clerics throughout the Khomeini years. Their purge began with the state institutions: the Islamic Guards, the Revolutionary Tribunals, and the Ministries of the Interior, Defense, Intelligence, Labor, and Heavy Industries. In presenting his first cabinet, Rafsanjani declared that he sought mainly "professional competence" and that he considered a prison sentence under the Pahlavi regime to be a "credit" but not a prerequisite. The purge was then extended to the Assembly of Experts in the form of a theological exam to test the scholastic competence of its candidates. Lo and behold, the exam was administered by the Guardian Council. Many radicals refused to take this demeaning exam, and of the few radicals who took it—such as Ayatollah Khalkhali, the notorious "hanging-judge"—most failed. Khalkhali had been qualified enough to preside as a judge and sentence to death hundreds of prisoners; but he was now deemed unqualified to sit in the Assembly of Experts.

Rafsanjani and Khamenei then purged Parliament itself—the last radical holdout. In preparation for the 1991 elections, Khamenei empowered the Guardian Council and the Interior Ministry— also in the hands of the moderates—with the authority to oversee the voting and scrutinize the qualifications of the candidates, especially their "practical commitment to the Leader and the Islamic Republic." In previous elections, Khomeini had eliminated candidates on the grounds of "lack of commitment to Islam." The spokesman for the Guardian Council announced that DDT was needed to cleanse Parliament of individuals with "difficult attitudes" (*^cavazi-ha*). Seventy-five radicals withdrew, forty were disqualified from running, and only a handful of the thirty radicals permitted to run managed to get elected.

Khalkhali declared that his candidacy had been rejected because rightists who had never participated in the revolution now controlled the Council of Guardians.[5] Behzad Navabi, the former minister of heavy industries, warned that the "true servants of the revolution, like himself, had been subjected to a political purge and would probably in the future face a physical purge."[6] Another disqualified candidate, who had earlier dismissed any talk of human rights as a foreign conspiracy, now complained that the Guardian Council had grossly violated the UN Covenant on Human Rights since it had failed to inform him of the charges brought against him, had given him insufficient time to respond, and had denied him the right to defend himself in a proper court of law.[7] The Guardian Council responded that in keeping confidentiality it had followed precedent, guarded "state secrets," and tried to protect the "public reputation" of the unqualified. The purged were expected to be grateful for this sensitivity.

These purges were relatively easy to carry out. For one thing, the extensive powers entrusted to the Leader left the radicals vulnerable. As Hojjat al-Islam Mohtashami, a leading radical, complained, the institution of *velayat-e faqih* was now being used as a club to beat revolutionary heads.[8] He added that he and his supporters believed in the concept of *velayat-e faqih*, as they had done ever since 1969, but this did not mean that all the decisions of the Supreme Faqih were devoid of error and tantamount to divine orders. Khomeini had issued his controversial 1988 decree on the powers of the state in order to strengthen the etatists against the laissez-faireists. Ironically, the same decree could now be cited to bolster the laissez-faireists against the etatists.

When the radicals complained that the Guardian Council was being misused, the moderates reminded them that the same institution had been used in the previous three elections to purge others, especially the secularists and the leftists.[9] When the radicals protested that they were being slandered as traitors, the moderates again reminded them that disobedience to the Leader was tantamount to disobedience to Allah. Ayatollah Azari-Qomi, a member of the Guardian Council, declared that those questioning the word of Leader Khamenei were proponents of "American Islam."[10] Another moderate argued that the opposition should not sit in Parliament, because they could not fully accept the constitutional oath, especially the clause requiring "obedience to the Vice-Regent of the Imam of the Age."[11]

Rafsanjani, Khamenei, and other moderates received support not only from the Guardian Council and the Assembly of Experts but also from the wealthy Anjuman-ha-ye Islami-ye Asnaf va Bazaar-e Tehran (Islamic Association of the Guilds and Bazaar of Tehran) and the influential Jam^{c}eh-e Modarresin-e Howzieh ^{c}El-mieh-e Qom (Society of the Seminary Teachers in Qom). The bazaar association financed parliamentary candidates and two major newspapers; *Resalat* (Divine message) and *Abrar* (The pious). *Resalat* was edited by the same former labor minister who had argued that the country did not need a labor law since it already had the Koran and upright Muslim employers. The seminary association supervised the network of Friday Sermon Preachers—a network it used to the hilt to campaign against the radical parliamentary candidates. The moderates also had the backing of a number of prominent ayatollahs, especially Golpayegani, Araki, Khoi, Marashi-Najafi, and Mahdavi-Kani. Even Ayatollah Montazeri, Khomeini's previous heir apparent, openly supported them. ,

Furthermore, the moderates effectively turned the populist rhetoric against the radicals themselves. The moderate deputies and Friday preachers, as well as *Resalat* and *Abrar*, waged an aggressive propaganda war against the "Mercedes-Benz mullas" and the *tabaqeh-e now keiseh* (newly moneyed class). They accused them of deceiving the oppressed, buying votes with unrealistic promises, misappropriating public funds, living in luxury, selling contraband, opening secret accounts in foreign banks, giving government contracts to their friends and relatives, and acting like a giant "octopus" that gives with one tentacle but takes with another.

They also placed responsibility for the country's malaise and social problems squarely on the shoulders of the radicals. They argued that a decade of etatism had widened the gap between rich and poor; stifled economic enterprise; increased crime, suicide, and drug addiction; caused runaway inflation; left over 90 percent of the population in poverty; failed to bring literacy to the masses; and compounded the horrendous housing shortage. Before the revolution, these problems had been blamed on the Pahlavis. Now they were blamed on the "extremist pseudoclerics." In the words of one deputy, the nation had the right to know how individuals paid 5 tomans per sermon can end up owning 15-million-toman Mercedes-Benzes.[12] "I have a question for the opposition," the deputy continued. "Have you not held key positions, especially ministries and judgeships, for the last ten years? Is not the country's economic plight the result of your misguided policies?" Of course, the moderates could always cite Khomeini on the importance of private property, law and order, and respect for the bazaars.

As the radicals have been marginalized, Rafsanjani and Khamenei have implemented a full range of Thermidor-type policies: in the economy, in social matters, in the judiciary, and in foreign affairs. In economic matters, they argue that the best way to help the masses is to encourage those with money to invest, since such investments will create jobs and raise the standard of living. This is strikingly similar to the Chicago school theory of trickle-down economics. They further argue that the revolution had been "guilty of excesses" and that it is time to put "aside childish ideas." Launching a new Five-Year Plan, Rafsanjani warned that the "worst mistake" a society can make is to consume more than it produces. "Some people," he declared, "claim that God will provide. But God provides only for those who work for their needs."[13] His speeches, as well as those of Khamenei, now emphasized "reconstruction," "realism," "work discipline," "managerial skills," "modern technology," "expertise and competence," "individual self-reliance," "entrepreneurship," and "stability." "To have social justice," Rafsanjani preached, "we must have a stable government. Only Marxists think that the state should wither away. Only our enemies accuse us of straying from the imam's line."[14] In another sermon, he claimed that the Islamic Republic was spending more on food subsidies than even Communist regimes, and that this was making citizens "overly dependent on the central government."[15]

The regime now openly declares its support for open-door and laissez-faire policies. It has relaxed price controls and import restrictions, lifted rationing from many goods, decreased subsidies for a number of commodities, reduced inflation by cutting back on expenditures, increased wage and salary differences, set up a stock exchange, narrowed the gap between the official and the black-market exchange rate for the dollar, encouraged the importation of consumer goods, reestablished free-trade zones in the Persian Gulf, and privatized over five hundred companies, factories, and agribusinesses that had been nationalized in 1979–80. What is more, the new Five-Year Plan calls for foreign investments totaling $27 billion.

To obtain external capital, the government has actively wooed expatriates who fled in 1979, signed agreements with the International Monetary Fund and the World Bank, and drastically liberalized the law on foreign investments. The law passed under the shah had stipulated that non-Iranians could own no more than 49 percent of any venture, and the Constitution of the Islamic Republic had "absolutely forbidden" all forms of foreign concessions and loans. But the new 1992 law—amending the constitution and the older law—lifts the 49 percent ceiling and permits foreigners to have total ownership of ventures and to export all their profits. In the words of Rafsanjani, "our most pressing goal is to convince the world that the country is ripe for foreign investments and loans."[16] This is a far cry from the days when the Khomeinists talked of "national self-sufficiency," land reform, nationalization of trade, "war profiteers," and "capitalist bloodsuckers."

In social policies, the regime has also changed direction. It has granted amnesty to wartime deserters and sold draft exemptions for $10,000 per person per three years. It has restored the name of Kermanshah; hailed Persepolis, the seat of the ancient monarchy, as part of the "national heritage"; placed the crown jewels, including the Peacock Throne, on public display—at least for those who can afford the exorbitant entry fee; returned to émigrés real estate "supervised" by the state since 1979; and annulled an earlier law permitting courts to rent to the poor apartments vacated by émigrés—it now argues that according to this false logic the state could expropriate all unused private cars. Moreover, it has launched an urban renewal program, and as in other countries, urban renewal often means poor removal. The bulldozing of shantytowns sparked off violent protests in 1992 in five major cities. The regime has aired Western and popular music and relaxed enforcement of the rules on full Islamic dress, permitting the use of cosmetics, colored chadors, and expensive Western clothes underneath. In a Friday sermon, Khamenei argued that God liked beauty, that Imam Hasan had worn decorative clothes when praying, and that Imam Ali had taken pride in the picturesque palm plantation he had cultivated outside Medina.[17] Imam Ali, the water carrier, was now depicted as a plantation owner.

The new social policies are most apparent in the regime's attitude to the population explosion. The regime had dismantled the shah's birth control clinics on the grounds that Islam and Iran needed a large population. Now, however, it argues that the 3.9 percent annual population growth—one of the highest in the world—is placing undue burdens on the country's scarce resources and social services. Besides, both Islam and Iran favor "healthy" families, that is, small ones. Declaring "one literate soldier is more precious than ten illiterate ones," the regime has distributed contraceptives, opened birth control clinics, cut subsidies to large households, and insisted that the ideal Muslim family should be limited to two children. On this as in other issues, Islam was interpreted according to expediency.

In judicial matters, the regime has promised that in the future defendants will be tried in "open courts" and can have defense attorneys. It has disbanded special courts set up to deal with so-called economic saboteurs (profiteers, speculators, and hoarders). It has amnestied some political prisoners, stopped televising public confessions, improved prison conditions, allowed international organizations to visit the main jail, and cut down on the number of political executions. This trend has led some observers to assume that economic liberalization will inevitably produce more political liberalization. But historians familiar with other nondemocratic regimes cannot be so confident that laissez-faire and political pluralism are inevitably linked. Besides, the continued use of terms such as "traitor," "foreign stooge," "vermin," and "mosquito," even against fellow clerics, diminishes the likelihood of attaining genuine liberalization in the near future. It was after all the moderate clerics who presided over the mass executions of political prisoners in 1988–89.

In foreign affairs, the shift to moderation has been very clear. Rafsanjani and Khamenei now stress that the revolution is not a commodity that can easily be exported; that the government should be "prudent," to avoid being tarred with the "terrorist" and "fanatical" brush; and that the way to inspire others is through economic rebuilding—this can be termed the Iranian version of Stalin's "Socialism in One Country." "The best way to export our revolution," declared Rafsanjani, "is to create conditions at home so that others will see the correctness of our path."[18]

When the Gulf War broke out, Iran refused to help Iraq and instead reestablished diplomatic ties with Britain and Saudi Arabia and improved relations with Egypt, the Gulf states, and some European countries. When the Shiis and Kurds in Iraq rose up in revolt, Iran failed to send help—even when Saddam Hosayn bombarded the holy cities of Najaf and Karbala. When the Communist regime in Kabul collapsed, Iran criticized the main Afghan Mojahedin guerrillas as "retrogressive," because their draft constitution disenfranchised women. When the Soviet Union disintegrated, Iran moved to establish cordial relations with the new Central Asian Republics, carefully avoiding religious propaganda that would alienate their secular and nationalistic elites. Iran's response to the fighting between Armenians and Azerbayjanis in Karabagh has been to come forward as an impartial mediator. Indeed, it has at times seemed to favor the Armenians. Clearly Armenia poses no threat, but an Azerbayjan allied to Turkey and talking of uniting with "southern Azerbayjan" is a serious threat to Iran.

As the Thermidor has accelerated, the radicals have had no choice but to bide their time and to denounce the "betrayal of the revolution" from the few forums still available to them—from their ever-diminishing parliamentary seats, from the few religious foundations controlled by them, and from their two newspapers, *Salam* (Peace) and *Bayan* (Explanation). They protest that those demanding blind allegiance to the present Leader are scheming to put aside the teachings of the Revolutionary Prophet. They charge that most of the new ministers and deputies had sat out the revolu-

tion whereas many of the purged militants had suffered for years
in the shah's torture chambers. One of them has complained that
"while we were in prison getting whipped and defending the
imam and Islam, many of our ministers were living comfortably
in England and North America. We know your pasts." "We demand," declared another, "laws that help the *mostazafin*. By
mostazafin we mean the deprived and barefooted masses who
supported the imam. We don't mean the capitalist leeches who
have crept into the revolution. We members of the clergy should
remember that we have enjoyed a good public reputation precisely because we have for a thousand years avoided luxury."[19]

The radicals warn that "medieval capitalists" are hiding behind
the turban and the concept of *velayat-e faqih;* that war profiteers,
not the state, are responsible for the current economic crisis; and
that laissez-faire policies will put yet more money into the pockets
of the "bloodsucking bazaar mafia" and thus make the situation
even more "explosive." "The sins of the bazaar," exclaimed one,
"especially hoarding and price gouging, cause the people to think
ill of the revolution, of the republic, of the imam, of the Koran,
and even of Islam."

They argue that the state has the duty to change the social
structure, teach the masses the benefits of collective labor, and
campaign against luxury, ostentation, selfishness, and individualism. The main goal should not be just to increase the gross national product but to improve income distribution, eradicate poverty, and equalize opportunities. "We must all live simple lives.
We must all live like the middle class." "The rich own villas and
apartment buildings and make millions in a few minutes wheeling
and dealing in the bazaar, whereas the poor working with their
hands continue to be deprived of housing and other basic necessi-
ties." "The imam always stressed that only those who have themselves experienced pain, poverty, and exploitation can represent
the masses."

The radicals tell the bazaars to keep out of politics and clerical
matters, practice honesty and religion in their daily lives, and
concentrate on doing what they are best at, namely, "buying and
selling beans and chick-peas." They declare that their opponents

are "more pro–free enterprise than even Western capitalists"; that they had earlier resisted income tax on the feeble grounds that such levies were not mentioned in the Koran; and that they were now spreading the "deadly poison" of consumerism, even covering posters in honor of the martyrs of the revolution with billboards advertising imported bananas. "We will establish true Islam," one deputy has declared, "when we sever the links between us clerics and all special interests, especially those hungry for money. Only then will we have a clergy capable of speaking properly on behalf of liberation, salvation, freedom, and the oppressed masses. So far we have replaced the monarchical feudal system with a clerical feudal system." Coming from a Khomeinist deputy, this last phrase speaks volumes.

One radical deputy has taken issue with the Friday preacher of Tehran who argued that Islam rejected the Marxist notion that the past was a history of class struggles. "Did not our imam," he has asked, "speak of the struggle between rich and poor? Did he not insist that today we have a war between the wealthy and the poor, between the oppressors and the oppressed, between the palace dwellers and the slum dwellers?" The whole ideological conflict has been summed up by Hojjat al-Islam Karrubi, the former Speaker of Parliament. Answering Ayatollah Azari-Qomi, who had stressed that according to Shii traditions the teachings of deceased senior clerics needed revising, Karrubi argues that Imam Khomeini had delivered a message valid for present and future generations: there is a continuous war between the rich and the poor and between "false" Islam, that of America and Saudi Arabia, which favors the oppressors, and "true" Islam, championed by the imam and the Islamic Revolution, which supports the oppressed. Some, he concludes, take quotations of the imam out of context, refuse to accept this central theme of his "eternal message," and, much like the Saudis, exploit religion to mislead and pacify the public. At the height of the Islamic Revolution, Khomeinists much like Karrubi had plastered the walls of Tehran with the unequivocal slogan: "Islam is not the opium of the masses." Perhaps the last laugh will be on the slogan writers, not on their intended target.

Notes

Introduction

1. See the summary of R. Wright's review of S. Arjomand's *The Turban for the Crown: The Islamic Revolution in Iran* (New York: Oxford University Press, 1988), in *New York Times,* 10 Dec. 1989. For R. Wright's own books, see her *Sacred Rage: The Wrath of Militant Islam* (New York: Simon and Schuster, 1985); and *In the Name of God: The Khomeini Decade* (New York: Simon and Schuster, 1989). These two books are remarkable in that they do not use a single Persian-language source. The equivalent would be an Iranian journalist writing two books on Reagan's America without using a single English-language source.

2. S. Arjomand, "A Victory for the Pragmatists," in *Islamic Fundamentalism and the Gulf Crisis,* ed. J. Piscatori (Chicago: American Academy of Arts and Sciences, 1991), pp. 52–69.

3. For discussions of Latin American populism, see M. Conniff, ed., *Latin American Populism in Comparative Perspective* (Albuquerque: University of New Mexico Press, 1982); C. Veliz, *Obstacles to Change in Latin America* (London: Oxford University Press, 1965); G. Germani, *Authoritarianism, Fascism, and National Populism* (New Brunswick: Transaction Books, 1978); G. Ionescu and E. Gellner, eds., *Populism* (London: Weinfeld and Nicolson, 1969); N. Mouzelis, "Ideology and Class Politics," *New Left Review* 112 (Nov.–Dec. 1978): 41–61; idem, "On the Concept of Populism," *Politics and Society* 14, no. 3 (1985): 329–48.

4. The few Western books that have looked at Khomeini's

works have tended to sanitize them, presumably to make them more palatable for Western tastes. E.g., see H. Algar, *Islam and Revolution: Writings and Declarations of Imam Khomeini* (Berkeley: Mizan Press, 1981); F. Rajaee, *Islamic Values and World View: Khomeyni on Man, the State and International Politics* (New York: University Press of America, 1983).

5. Khomeini's birth certificate—issued years later—gives his birth date as 1900. But, according to Ayatollah Pasandideh, Khomeini's elder brother, the correct date is 1902. See Ayatollah Pasandideh, "The Life of the Leader of the Revolution," *Iran Times*, 17 Mar.–19 May 1989.

6. Ibid.

7. H. Ruhani, *Nahzat-e Imam Khomeini* (Imam Khomeini's movement) (Tehran: Imam's Way Press, 1984), vol. 1, pp. 20–22.

8. Y. Dawlatabadi, *Hayat-e Yahya* (Life of Yahya) (Tehran: Ibn Sina Press, 1949), vol. 3, pp. 287–89.

9. For an attempt to date these early manuscripts, see M. Vajdani, ed., *Sarguzashtha-ye Vezhah az Zindegani-e Hazrat Imam Khomeini* (Special reminiscencies from the life of His Excellency Imam Khomeini) (Tehran: Payam-e Azadi Press, 1982), vol. 1, pp. 139–49; M. Fahimi, "The Bibliography of His Excellency Imam Khomeini," *Kayhan-e Farhangi* 6, no. 3 (June 1989): 12–17; and anonymous, "Imam Khomeini's Publications," *Kayhan-e Hava'i*, 5 June 1991.

10. A. Ali-Babai, "Open Letter to Khomeini," *Iranshahr*, 15 June–16 July 1982.

11. Pasandideh, "The Life," *Iran Times*, 21 Apr. 1989.

12. Vajdani, *Sarguzashtha-ye Vezhah*, vol. 3, p. 19.

13. "Interview with Dr. Bahonar," *Jomhuri-ye Islami*, 19 Dec. 1979.

14. Vajdani, *Sarguzashtha-ye Vezhah*, vol. 2, p. 47.

15. M. Busheri, "From *Secrets Unveiled* to *Thousand Year Secrets*," *Cheshmandaz*, no. 6 (Summer 1989): 14–26.

16. Vajdani, *Sarguzashtha-ye Vezhah*, vol. 1, p. 144.

17. Ibid., vol. 2, p. 25.

18. For the proclamations against the White Revolution, see A. Davani, *Nahzat-e Ruhaniyun-e Iran* (The movement of the Iranian clergy) (Qom: Imam Reza Foundation, 1981), vol. 3.

19. For Khomeini's decree against the referendum, see Ruhani, *Nahzat-e Imam Khomeini*, vol. 1, pp. 230–31.

20. Vajdani, *Sarguzashtha-ye Vezhah*, vol. 4, pp. 86–87.

21. Front for the Liberation of the Iranian People (JAMA), *Khomeini va Jonbesh* (Khomeini and the movement) (N.p.: Moharram Press, 1973), pp. 1–118.

22. Vajdani, *Sarguzashtha-ye Vezhah*, vol. 6, p. 110.

23. Khomeini used translators when communicating with Arabs. See ibid., p. 133.

24. For the pronouncements before 1979, see Front for the Liberation of the Iranian People (JAMA), *Majmu^ceh az Maktubat, Sukhanrani-ha, Payham-ha, va Raftari-ha-ye Imam Khomeini* (Collection from Imam Khomeini's teachings, speeches, messages, and activities) (Tehran: Chapkhesh Press, n.d.); and the newspapers *Khabarnameh*, 1972–78; *Payam-e Mojahed*, 1972–78; and *Bakhtar-e Emruz*, 1972–78. For the press interviews, see Tehran University Publication Center, *Mosahebeh-ha-ye Imam Khomeini dar Najaf, Paris, va Qom* (Imam Khomeini's interviews in Najaf, Paris, and Qom) (Tehran: Tehran University Press, 1981).

25. For the post-1978 pronouncements, see the newspapers *Kayhan, Kayhan-e Hava'i, Ettela^cat, Jomhuri-ye Islami, Iran Times,* and *Tehran Times.*

Chapter 1. Fundamentalism or Populism?

1. R. Khomeini, *Kashf al-Asrar* (Secrets unveiled) (Tehran: N.p., 1943), p. 322. See also Khomeini's speeches in *Jomhuri-ye Islami*, 22–31 Dec. 1979; *Ettela^cat*, 25 Aug. 1986 and 18 Nov. 1987; *Kayhan-e Hava'i*, 18 Nov. 1987. For his most overtly mystical writing, see R. Khomeini, letter to Fatemeh Tabatabai, *Kayhan-e Hava'i*, 23–30 May 1990. For a brief analysis of the influence of mysticism on Khomeini, see N. Pakdaman, "Until the Death of Khomeinism," *Cheshmandaz*, no. 6 (Summer 1989): 1–13. Ahmad Khomeini, his son, published a short poem Khomeini had composed just before his death full of the usual clichés and language found in traditional Sufi poetry, including the obligatory homage to al-Hallaj, the tenth-century mystic who

was executed for his heretic notion that mortals could merge with God. See *Kayhan,* 21 June 1989.

2. R. Khomeini, speech, *Ettela^{C}at,* 28 Dec. 1979; *Kayhan-e Hava'i,* 9 May 1984.

3. R. Khomeini, speech, *Iran Times,* 4 Dec. 1982.

4. S. Zubaida, *Islam, the People and the State* (London: Routledge, 1989), pp. 1–37.

5. Cited by S. Bakhash, "Islam and Social Justice in Iran," in *Shi^{C}ism, Resistance, and Revolution,* ed. M. Kramer (Boulder: Westview Press, 1987), p. 113.

6. R. Khomeini, *Velayat-e Faqih: Hokumat-e Islami* (The jurist's guardianship: Islamic government) (Tehran: N.p., 1978), pp. 13–14.

7. H. Rafsanjani, speech, *Kayhan-e Hava'i,* 20 Dec. 1987.

8. M. Hojjati-Kermani, "The Jurisprudent and Modern Civilization," *Ettela^{C}at,* 4 Nov.–5 Dec. 1988.

9. Ibid.

10. See, e.g., S. Arjomand, "Traditionalism in Twentieth-century Iran," in *From Nationalism to Revolutionary Islam,* ed. S. Arjomand (Albany: State University of New York Press, 1984), pp. 195–232.

11. One early nineteenth-century cleric, Ahmad Naraqi, made implicit claims that the clergy had authority over the shahs, but he did not define this authority or make explicit political claims. See H. Dabashi, "Early Propagation of Wilayat-i Faqih," in *Expectations of the Millennium,* ed. H. Nasr, H. Dabashi, and V. Nasr (Albany: State University of New York Press, 1989), pp. 288–300.

12. Khomeini, *Kashf al-Asrar,* pp. 1–66.

13. Ibid., pp. 185–88.

14. Ibid., p. 226.

15. Ibid., p. 195.

16. Vajdani, *Sarguzashtha-ye Vezhah,* vol. 4, p. 121.

17. For Khomeini's speeches and proclamations in these years, especially 1962–64, see Ruhani, *Nahzat-e Imam Khomeini,* vol. 1, pp. 142–735; Front for the Liberation of the Iranian People, *Khomeini va Jonbesh,* pp. 1–35.

18. Ruhani, *Nahzat-e Imam Khomeini,* vol. 1, p. 195.

19. Ibid., p. 198.

20. Ibid., p. 458.

21. Ibid., vol. 2, p. 159.

22. One such theologian was Ayatollah Mohammad Baqer Sadr, who published a treatise in which he tried to prove that Islam had a radical economic theory and that this theory was superior to that of all other systems of thought, including socialism. Even though Khomeini and Baqer Sadr were not on good terms, the latter's works were well known among the former's students in Najaf. See H. Akhavan-Tawhidi (pseud.), *Dar Pas-e Pardeh-e Tazvir* (Behind the veils of dissimulation) (Paris: N.p., 1984), pp. 111–13.

23. E. Hooglund, "Social Origins of the Revolutionary Clergy," in *The Iranian Revolution and the Islamic Republic*, ed. N. Keddie and E. Hooglund (Syracuse: Syracuse University Press, 1986), pp. 74–90.

24. On al-Ahmad, see R. Mottahedeh, *The Mantle of the Prophet* (New York: Simon and Schuster, 1985), pp. 287–315.

25. Mehdi Bazargan's supporters argued that the Khomeinists had been influenced by radical intellectuals. See Liberation Movement of Iran, *Mavaze^C-e Nahzat-e Azadi Darbarabar-e Enqelab-e Islami* (The issue of the Liberation Movement being against the Islamic Republic) (Tehran: Liberation Movement Press, 1982), p. 143.

26. Khomeini, *Velayat-e Faqih*, pp. 177–79.

27. Vajdani, *Sarguzashtha-ye Vezhah*, vol. 1, p. 99.

28. A. Khomeini, proclamation, *Khabarnameh*, Sept.–Oct. 1970.

29. *Mojahed*, 28 Feb. 1975.

30. R. Khomeini, speech, *Ettela^Cat*, 2 Dec. 1985.

31. Khomeini, *Velayat-e Faqih*, pp. 76–127.

32. Ibid., p. 85.

33. R. Khomeini, speech, *Ettela^Cat*, 16 June 1981. See also *Ettela^Cat*, 10 Jan. 1981; and *Kayhan-e Hava'i*, 1 Mar. 1989.

34. Enqelab is used in a favorable sense in only one place in the whole of *Velayat-e Faqih* (p. 41), probably indicating that it was inserted by his students, who actually published the work.

35. R. Namvar, *Yadnameh-e Shahidan* (Martyrs' memorial) (N.p.: Tudeh Party Press, 1964), pp. 1–63.

36. Mojahedin, *Nahzat-e Hosayni* (Hosayn's movement) (Springfield, Mo.: Liberation Movement Press, 1976).

37. A. Shariati, *Shahadat* (Martyrdom) (Tehran: Hosaynieh-e Ershad Press, 1972).

38. R. Khomeini, speech, *Ettela^{C}at*, 8 Sept. 1982.

39. S. Najafabadi, *Shahid-e Javid* (The eternal martyr) (Tehran: Forough Danesh Press, 1981).

40. Liberation Movement, *Velayat-e Motlaqah-e Faqih* (The jurist's absolute guardianship) (Tehran: Liberation Movement Press, 1988).

41. Ruhani, *Nahzat-e Imam Khomeini*, vol. 2, p. 512.

42. Personal communications from Dr. Mansur Farhang, the former Iranian representative at the United Nations.

43. For Khomeini's speeches on these issues, see Ruhani, *Nahzat-e Imam Khomeini*, vol. 1; Front for the Liberation of the Iranian People, *Khomeini va Jonbesh; Khabarnameh*, 1972–79; *Payam-e Mojahed*, 1972–78.

44. For examples of the use of such slogans, see "The Oppressors and the Oppressed," *Ettela^{C}at*, 15 Feb.–23 Apr. 1983. See also Tudeh Party, *Hezb-e Tudeh-e Iran az Khatt-e Imam Poshtebani Mekonad* (The Tudeh party of Iran supports Imam Khomeini's line) (Tehran: Tudeh Party Press, 1979), pp. 1–32.

45. R. Khomeini, speech, *Iran Times*, 27 May 1983.

46. R. Khomeini, speech, *Ettela^{C}at*, 13 Apr. 1988; *Iran Times*, 27 Mar. 1982.

47. For a complete text of the constitution, see *Iran Times*, 30 Nov. 1979. For later revisions, see *Kayhan-e Hava'i*, 19 June 1989.

48. A. Moussavi, "A New Interpretation of the Theory of *Velayat-e Faqih*," *Middle Eastern Studies* 28, no. 1 (Jan. 1992): 101–7.

49. R. Khomeini, speech, *Kayhan-e Hava'i*, 1 Mar. 1989.

50. For discussion of the controversial term "imam," see M. Fischer, "Imam Khomeini: Four Levels of Understanding," in *Voices of Resurgent Islam*, ed. J. Esposito (New York: Oxford

University Press, 1983), p. 164; Arjomand, *The Turban for the Crown*, p. 101.

51. R. Khomeini, *Matn-e Kamel-e Vasiyatnameh-e Elahi va Siyasi-ye Imam Khomeini* (The complete text of Imam Khomeini's divine will and political testament), *Kayhan-e Hava'i*, 14 June 1989.

Chapter 2. Perceptions of Private Property, Society, and the State

1. For depiction of Khomeini as a "socialistic" radical, see E. Kedourie, "Crisis and Revolution in Modern Islam," *Times Literary Supplement*, 19–25 May 1989; H. Enayat, "Iran: Khumayni's Concept of the 'Guardianship of the Juristconsult,' " in *Islam in the Political Process*, ed. J. Piscatori (New York: Cambridge University Press, 1983), pp. 160–80; R. Savory, "Ex Oriente Nebula," in *Ideology and Power in the Middle East*, ed. P. Chelkowski and R. Pranger (Durham, N.C.: Duke University Press, 1988), pp. 339–64; and N. Calder, "Accommodation and Revolution in Imami Shi^{C}i Jurisprudence," *Middle Eastern Studies* 18, no. 1 (Jan. 1982): 3–20.

2. Khomeini, *Kashf al-Asrar*, pp. 181–82, 229–30, 282, 289–91.

3. Ibid., p. 259.

4. Ibid., pp. 266–67.

5. Y. Richard, "Shari^{C}at Sangalaji: A Reformist Theologian," in *Authority and Political Culture in Shi^{C}ism*, ed. S. Arjomand (Albany: State University of New York Press, 1988), p. 160.

6. R. Khomeini, *Towzih al-Masa'el* (Questions clarified) (Tehran: N.p., 1978), p. 133.

7. Ibid., p. 408.

8. Khomeini, *Velayat-e Faqih*, p. 52.

9. Ruhani, *Nahzat-e Imam Khomeini*, vol. 2, p. 272.

10. R. Khomeini, sermon at Large Mosque in Qom, reprinted in Front for the Liberation of the Iranian People, *Khomeini va Jonbesh*, p. 9.

11. Ibid., pp. 30–31.

12. Ruhani, *Nahzat-e Imam Khomeini*, vol. 2, p. 217.

13. Ibid., p. 701.

14. Tehran University Publication Center, *Mosahebeh-ha-ye Imam Khomeini*, p. 303.

15. R. Khomeini, "Announcement against Anarchy," *Ettela^cat*, 12 Dec. 1979.

16. R. Khomeini, speech on major conflicts, *Ettela^cat*, 7 July 1979.

17. R. Khomeini, speech to the Islamic judges, *Ettela^cat*, 16 Oct. 1979.

18. R. Khomeini, "The People Do Not Want an Oppressive Government," *Ettela^cat*, 30 Sept. 1979.

19. R. Khomeini, "The Blood of the Martyrs," *Ettela^cat*, 29 Dec. 1980.

20. R. Khomeini, speech to provincial governors, *Ettela^cat*, 7 Dec. 1980.

21. R. Khomeini, "On Spreading the Revolution," *Ettela^cat*, 23 Mar. 1980.

22. R. Khomeini, speech to the Tehran guilds, *Ettela^cat*, 17 Jan. 1981.

23. R. Khomeini, speech to the municipal political-ideological leaders, *Ettela^cat*, 24 Feb. 1981.

24. R. Khomeini, "Eight-Point Declaration," *Ettela^cat*, 16 Dec. 1981.

25. R. Khomeini, speech, *Iran Times*, 13 Aug. 1982.

26. R. Khomeini, "The Government Stands Firm," *Ettela^cat*, 31 Jan. 1982.

27. R. Khomeini, speech, *Iran Times*, 24 Dec. 1982.

28. R. Khomeini, "If We Want Islam, We Must Preserve This Republic," *Tehran Times*, 14 Apr. 1982.

29. A. Khomeini, "The Complete Text of Imam Khomeini's Last Will and Political Testament," *Kayhan-e Hava'i*, 14 June 1989.

30. M. Beheshti, "Islam and Private Property," reprinted in *Kayhan-e Hava'i*, 4 July–1 Aug. 1990.

31. Special Issue for the Memory of Martyr-Teacher Morteza Motahhari, *Ettela^cat*, 2 May 1984.

32. M. Motahhari, *Jahanbeni-ye Islami* (Islam's world out-

look) (Albany, Calif.: Muslim Student Association in America Press, 1980), vols. 1–3. See also A. Abu al-Hoseyni, *Shahid Motahhari* (The martyr Motahhari) (Qom: Howzieh-e ^CElmieh-e Qom Press, 1984).

33. R. Khomeini, speech, *Ettela^Cat*, 20 July 1983. See also "Interview with Imam Khomeini," *Jomhuri-ye Islami*, 2 Jan. 1980.

34. For the links between private property, natural law, and political liberalism, see C. Macpherson, *The Political Theory of Possessive Individualism* (Oxford: Oxford University Press, 1962).

35. Khomeini, *Velayat-e Faqih*, pp. 26–35, 45–46, 180–81.

36. I. Berlin, *The Crooked Timber of Humanity: Chapters in the History of Ideas* (New York: Knopf, 1991).

37. A. Moussavi, "A New Interpretation of the Theory of *Velayat-e Faqih*," pp. 101–7.

38. S. Ossowski, *Class Structure in Social Consciousness* (London: Routledge and Kegan Paul, 1979), pp. 38–53.

39. Khomeini, *Kashf al-Asrar*, p. 255. See also Ruhani, *Nahzat-e Imam Khomeini*, vol. 1, pp. 656, 724.

40. Khomeini, *Towzih al-Masa'el*, pp. 131, 334.

41. Ibid., p. 11.

42. Ruhani, *Nahzat-e Imam Khomeini*, vol. 1, p. 742.

43. For a compilation of Khomeini's 1970–82 speeches using such imagery, see "The Oppressors and the Oppressed," *Ettela^Cat*, 15 Feb.–23 Apr. 1983.

44. Khomeini, *Velayat-e Faqih*, pp. 42–43.

45. R. Khomeini, "The People Do Not Want an Oppressive Government," *Ettela^Cat*, 30 Sept. 1979.

46. Ossowski, *Class Structure in Social Consciousness*, pp. 19–37.

47. Front for the Liberation of the Iranian People, *Khomeini va Jonbesh;* Ruhani, *Nahzat-e Imam Khomeini*, vol. 1, pp. 316–18, 413, 417, 459, 656; vol. 2, p. 232, 234, 235, 236, 237, 243, 598, 607–8; Khomeini, *Velayat-e Faqih*, pp. 6–7, 38, 175.

48. R. Khomeini, "I Want to Take from the Foreigners and the Rich and Give to the Poor," *Ettela^Cat*, 19 June 1979.

49. R. Khomeini, speech to the Islamic Student Association, *Ettela^Cat*, 28 June 1979.

50. R. Khomeini, speech to Kuwaiti visitors, *Ettela^Cat*, 26 Aug. 1979.

51. Vajdani, *Sarguzashtha-ye Vezhah*, vols. 1–6.

52. After a brief stay in Qom, Khomeini returned to Tehran and spent the last nine years of his life in a fortress-like house in one of the more expensive northern suburbs.

53. R. Khomeini, "The Report Card on Jews Differs from That on the Zionists," *Ettela^Cat*, 11 May 1979.

54. Ibid.

55. R. Khomeini, "We Need a Spiritual Revolution in Iran," *Ettela^Cat*, 19 July 1979.

56. R. Khomeini, speech to bazaaris and factory owners, *Ettela^Cat*, 7 July 1979.

57. R. Khomeini, speech to clerics from Qom," *Kayhan-e Hava'i*, 15 May 1985.

58. R. Khomeini, speech, *Jomhuri-ye Islami*, 12 Feb. 1982.

59. R. Khomeini, "The State Must Help the People," *Kayhan-e Hava'i*, 5 Sept. 1984.

60. R. Khomeini, speech on the anniversary of the 1963 uprising, *Iran Times*, 20 June 1982.

61. R. Khomeini, speech for the parliamentary elections, *Iran Times*, 2 Jan. 1984.

62. A. Rafsanjani, Friday sermon, *Kayhan-e Hava'i*, 22 Apr. 1987.

63. For diverse uses of the term, see S. Shafi^Ci, "Who Is a Mostazaf?" *Kayhan*, 26 July 1986.

64. R. Khomeini, speech to the parliamentary deputies, *Ettela^Cat*, 9 Feb. 1982.

65. R. Khomeini, speeches, *Ettela^Cat*, 10 Jan. 1980, 16 Mar. 1980, 26 Apr. 1980.

66. R. Khomeini, speech to government officials, *Ettela^Cat*, 25 Jan. 1984.

67. R. Khomeini, speech to Tehran merchants and guildsmen, *Ettela^Cat*, 17 Jan. 1981.

68. A. Khamenei, speech, *Iran Times*, 18 Dec. 1988.

69. Khomeini, *Kashf al-Asrar*, pp. 181–82; see also idem, *Velayat-e Faqih*, pp. 32–34, 46.

70. R. Khomeini, speech, *Ettela^Cat*, 26 Mar. 1983.

71. R. Khomeini, speech, *Iran Times*, 31 Aug. 1984.

72. R. Khomeini, "The State Must Let the People Participate in Trade, Industry, and Agriculture," *Kayhan-e Hava'i*, 5 Sept. 1984.

73. R. Khomeini, speech, *Ettela^Cat*, 3 Jan. 1984.

74. R. Khomeini, speech to Tehran merchants and guildsmen, *Ettela^Cat*, 17 Jan. 1981.

75. R. Khomeini, speech to bazaaris and factory owners, *Ettela^Cat*, 7 July 1979.

76. R. Khomeini, "Government Is an Absolute Authority Entrusted by Divinity to the Prophet," *Kayhan-e Hava'i*, 19 Jan. 1988.

77. Liberation Movement, *Velayat-e Motlaqeh-e Faqih* (The jurist's absolute guardianship) (Tehran: Liberation Movement Press, 1988).

78. Khomeini, *Velayat-e Faqih*, p. 52.

79. For the Sunni concept of public interest, see M. Kamali, *The Principles of Islamic Jurisprudence* (New York: Cambridge University Press, 1991), pp. 267–81.

80. Khomeini, *Vasiyatnameh-e Elahi va Siyasi*, p. 7.

Chapter 3. May Day in the Islamic Republic

1. For the concept of "invented tradition," see E. Hobsbawm and T. Ranger, eds., *The Invention of Traditions* (New York: Cambridge University Press, 1985).

2. For recent literature on May Day, see A. Panaccione, *May Day Celebration* (Venice: Marsilio Editori, 1988); E. Hobsbawm, "100 Years of May Day," *Times Literary Supplement*, 14 May 1990; C. Wrigley, "May Days and After," *History Today*, June 1990, pp. 35–42; P. Foner, *May Day* (New York: International Publishers, 1986).

3. S. Mani, *Tarikhcheh-e Nahzat-e Kargari dar Iran* (Short history of the labor movement in Iran) (Tehran: Taban Press,

1946), pp. 1–25; M. Nashehi, "Workers' Organizations in Iran,"
Rahbar, 10 Apr. 1944; R. Rusta, "The Central Council of Feder-
ated Trade Unions," *Razm Mahnameh* 1 (June 1946): 62–64; A.
Ovanessian, "Reminiscences of the Communist Party of Iran,"
Donya 3, no. 1 (Spring 1962): 33–34; idem, *Safahat-e Chand az
Jonbesh-e Kargari va Komunisti-ye Iran dar Dawreh-e Aval-e
Saltanat-e Reza Shah* (A few pages from the history of the work-
ers' and Communist movement in Iran during the early years of
Reza Shah's rule) (N.p.: Tudeh Party Press, 1979), pp. 1–140; P.
Mehrban, "Memoirs of Comrade Yasari," *Donya* 2, no. 7 (Sept.–
Oct. 1980): 126–32; F. Qassemi, *Sindykalism dar Iran* (Syndical-
ism in Iran) (Paris: Mosaddeq Publishing Foundation, 1985),
vol. 1.

4. In 1920 the Armenian Social Democratic Hunchak
Party—a former affiliate of the Russian Social Democratic
Party—had organized an indoor May Day meeting in its Tabriz
clubhouse. This meeting, however, was intended for the Armenian community alone; the announcement was in Armenian,
and the meeting was conducted in Armenian. See Hunchak Party,
"May Day Manifesto," reprinted in K. Shakeri, ed., *Asnad-e
Tarikhi: Jonbesh-e Kargari, Sosiyal Democrasi va Komunisti-ye
Iran* (Historical documents: The Workers', Social Democratic,
and Communist movement in Iran) (Florence: Mazdak Press,
1982), vol. 2, pp. 141–43. This volume has a useful collection of
early May Day manifestos.

5. Editorial, "May First," *Haqiqat*, 28 Apr. 1922. Reprinted
in Shakeri, *Asnad-e Tarikhi*, vol. 7.

6. A. Ovanessian, "Some Reminiscences of the Toilers' University in Moscow," *Donya* 9, no. 1 (Spring 1969): 97.

7. British Legation to the Foreign Office, 19 Dec. 1928, PRO,
FO 371/Persia 1929/34-13783.

8. A. Ovanessian, "Reminiscences of the Communist Party in
Khorasan," *Donya* 6, no. 3 (Autumn 1965): 81–82.

9. A. Ovanessian, "Reminiscences of the Communist Party in
Tehran," *Donya* 7, no. 3 (Autumn 1966): 116–19. See also idem,
Safahat-e Chand, pp. 20–21.

10. Communist Party, "May Day Manifesto (1928)," reprinted
in Shakeri, *Asnad-e Tarikhi*, vol. 6, pp. 123–24.

11. Ovanessian, "Reminiscences of the Communist Party in Tehran."

12. Ovanessian, "Reminiscences of the Communist Party in Khorasan," *Donya* 6, no. 3 (Autumn 1965): 78. Local intellectuals, especially teachers, had unionized the carpet weavers with the help of adult literacy classes and football games. In fact, football was introduced in Iran in the 1920s through socialist and communist clubhouses.

13. "Fifty Years of the Oil Workers' Struggle," *Mardom* 6, no. 7 (Sept.–Oct. 1964); L. P. Elwell-Sutton, *Persian Oil* (London: Lawrence and Wishart, 1955), pp. 68–69; British Legation to the Foreign Office, "May Day Parade in Abadan," PRO, FO 371/Persia 1929/34-13783; Ovanessian, *Safahat-e Chand*, pp. 78–81.

14. Foreign office to the British Legation in Tehran, 4 May 1929, PRO, FO 371/Persia 1929/34-13783.

15. Lt. Col. Barrett to the Foreign Office, "Bolshevik Activity in the South," PRO, FO 371/Persia 1929/34-13783.

16. Mani, *Tarikhcheh-e*, pp. 21–23.

17. "Short History of Trade Unions in Isfahan," *Rahbar*, 18 June 1944.

18. Ovanessian, *Safahat-e Chand*, p. 119.

19. R. Namvar, *Yadnameh-e Shahidan* (Martyrs' memorial) (N.p.: Tudeh Publications, 1964), p. 11.

20. T. Arani, "May Day Manifesto," reprinted in *Iran-e Ma*, 1 May 1946.

21. For a survey of new factories, see W. Floor, *Industrialization in Iran* (Durham, England: Center for Middle Eastern Studies, 1984).

22. British Labor Attaché to the Foreign Office, "The Tudeh Party and the Iranian Trade Unions," PRO, FO 371/Persia 1947/34-61993.

23. *Zafar*, 3 May 1946.

24. A. Natefi, "May 1: Ardibehesht 11," *Zafar*, 6–18 May 1946.

25. D. Wilber, *Adventures in the Middle East* (Princeton: Darwin Press, 1986), p. 121.

26. *Zafar*, 14 May 1946.

27. British Embassy to the Foreign Office, "Memorandum on Tudeh Activities against the Anglo-Iranian Oil Company," PRO, FO 371/Persia 1946/34-52713.

28. British Consul in Ahwaz to the Foreign Office, Report for June 1946, PRO, FO 371/Persia 34-52700.

29. Colonel Underwood, "Report on Tudeh Activities in the Oil Industry," PRO, FO 371/Persia 1946/34-52714.

30. British Cabinet, 4 July 1946, PRO, FO 371/Persia 1946/34-52706.

31. For an excellent description of labor under the shah, see H. Ladjevardi, *Labor Unions and Autocracy in Iran* (Syracuse: Syracuse University Press, 1985). See also T. Jalil, *Workers Say No to the Shah* (London: Campaign for the Restoration of Trade Union Rights in Iran, 1977); and A. Fischer, "The Labour Movement in Iran," *Contemporary Review* (Apr. 1977): 209–12.

32. *Kar*, 1 May 1980.

33. For the use of weddings as a cover, see Editorial, "May 1: Day of International Solidarity," *Kar*, 30 Apr. 1979.

34. "Interview with Comrade Worker Hajj Tehrani," *Kar*, 30 Apr. 1981.

35. Central Bank of Iran, *Natayej-e Barresi-ye Kargahha-ye Bozorg-e Sanati-ye Keshvar dar Sal-e 1356* (The results of an investigation into large manufacturing plants in the country in the year 1977) (Tehran: Government Publishing House, 1978). I would like to thank Dr. Parvin Alizadeh for making this report available to me.

36. N. Pakdaman, "Labor Unions," *Ayandegan*, 2 May 1979.

37. For two excellent studies of urban migration, see F. Kazemi, *Poverty and Revolution in Iran* (New York: New York University Press, 1980); and P. Vieille, *Psycho-sociologie du travail industriel en Iran* (Paris: Institute of Sociological Research of Tehran, 1965).

38. W. Bartsch, "Unemployment in Less Developed Countries: A Case Study of a Poor District of Tehran," *International Development Review*, 1975, no. 1, pp. 19–22.

39. The government apparently toyed with the idea of having a Labor Day on the shah's birthday but eventually decided against

it. See "Interview with Comrade Worker Hajj Tehrani," *Kar*, 30 Apr. 1981.

40. H. Hakimian, "Industrialization and the Standard of Living of the Working Class in Iran, 1960–79," *Development and Change* 19, no. 1 (Jan. 1988): 3–32.

41. *Ettela^{C}at*, 1 May 1974.

42. *Ettela^{C}at*, 1 May 1975.

43. *Talesh*, 7 May 1975.

44. *Ettela^{C}at*, 1 May 1976.

45. *Ettela^{C}at*, 2 May 1977.

46. E. Rouleau, "Les tensions politique en Iran," *Le monde*, 2 May 1979.

47. A. Khomeini, May Day speech, *Ettela^{C}at*, 2 May 1979.

48. *Azadi*, 2 May 1979.

49. Society of Tehran Clerics, "May Day Message," *Ettela^{C}at*, 1 May 1979.

50. *Azadi*, 2 May 1979.

51. Rouleau, "Tensions politique en Iran."

52. C. Goodey, "Workers' Councils in Iranian Factories," *Merip* 88 (June 1980): 3–9.

53. Ibid.

54. Rouleau, "Tensions politique en Iran."

55. Special Correspondent, "Thousands Parade in Iran," *New York Times*, 2 May 1979.

56. *Ayandegan*, 2 May 1979.

57. For example, see the poems "May 1," in *Mardom*, 3 May 1979; "Forward," in *Kar*, 30 Apr. 1979; "This Is Our Festival," in *Kar*, 30 Apr. 1979; and "Workers' Day," in *Ahangar*, 1 May 1979.

58. *Ettela^{C}at*, 2 May 1979.

59. N. Tabandeh, "Workers' Day," *Ettela^{C}at*, 8 May 1980.

60. A. Khomeini, May Day speech, *Ettela^{C}at*, 3 May 1980.

61. H. Musavi-Khoeiniha, speech outside the American Embassy, *Jomhuri-ye Islami*, 3 May 1980.

62. *Mardom*, 3 May 1980.

63. *Mardom*, 1 May 1980.

64. *Ettela^{C}at*, 30 Apr. 1980.

65. For coverage of May Day 1982, see *Kar*, 6 May 1982. Pictures show that the Majority Fedayin filled Liberation Square. Hezbollahis attacked and injured ten, including a four-year-old girl.

66. *Ettela^{C}at*, 1 May 1983.

67. H. Kamali, speech to Parliament, *Iranshahr*, 9 May 1982.

68. "Programs for International Workers' Day," *Kar va Kargar*, 8 May 1990.

69. A. Montazeri, May Day speech, *Ettela^{C}at*, 1 May 1982. See also *Ettela^{C}at*, 4 May 1985.

70. *Ettela^{C}at*, 4 May 1985.

71. A. Khomeini, May Day speech, *Iran Times*, 2 May 1982.

Chapter 4. History Used and Abused

1. These public confessions were printed with much fanfare in the mass media, especially in *Ettela^{C}at*, beginning on 1 May 1983 and ending on 17 January 1984. Like the famous Moscow and Slansky show trials of the 1930s and 1950s, these public confessions fueled much speculation. Royalists dismissed them as a smokescreen designed to hide from the West the Islamic Republic's true intention—an alliance with the Soviet Union. The Mojahedin exclaimed that the confessions proved once again their long-standing charge that the Tudeh leaders were "opportunistic," "self-seeking," and "unscrupulous." Other leftists argued that the Tudeh had already moved so close to the Islamic Republic that a gentle nudge was enough to push it completely into the clerical camp. The Tudeh itself claimed that its leaders had been brainwashed through mind-altering drugs supplied by Mossad, MI5, and the CIA. Once the dust settled, however, it became clear that the authorities had obtained these confessions through more direct methods—through brute physical force. Evidence of physical torture, including crushed fingers and hands, was later provided by the first secretary of the Tudeh party. See R. Galindo (Special UN Representative of the Commission on Human Rights), *Report on the Human Rights Situation in the Islamic*

Republic of Iran (New York: UN, Economic and Social Council, 1990), pp. 32, 42.

2. M. Rezvani, "Shaykh Fazlollah Nuri's Newspaper," *Tarikh* 1, no. 2 (1977): 159–209.

3. On Shaykh Fazlollah Nuri, see A. Kasravi, *Tarikh-e Mashruteh-ye Iran* (History of the constitutional movement in Iran) (Tehran: Amir Kaber Press, 1961), pp. 415–27; H. Rezvani, *Lavayeh-e Aqa-ye Shaykh Fazlollah Nuri* (Shaykh Fazlollah Nuri's essays) (Tehran: Naqsh-e Jahan Press, 1982); M. Turkoman, *Shaykh-e Shahid Fazlollah Nuri* (Martyred Shaykh Fazlollah Nuri) (Tehran: 1983); V. Martin, *Islam and Modernism* (Syracuse: Syracuse University Press, 1989); A. Arjomand, "The Ulama's Traditionalist Opposition to Parliamentarianism, *Middle Eastern Studies* 17, no. 2 (Apr. 1981): 174–89.

4. I. Afshar, ed., *Yaddashtha-ye Tarikhi-ye Mostasher al-Dawleh* (The political memoirs of Mostasher al-Dawleh) (Tehran: Ramin Press, 1982), pp. 76–82.

5. Khomeini, *Velayat-e Faqih*, pp. 10–11.

6. R. Khomeini, speech, *Ettela^{C}at*, 27 Nov. 1983; *Kayhan-e Hava'i*, 21 Dec. 1983.

7. R. Khomeini, speech, *Ettela^{C}at*, 3 Jan. 1984.

8. A. Mahdavi-Kani, speech, *Ettela^{C}at*, 7 May 1983.

9. J. al-Ahmad, *Gharbzadegi* (The plague from the West) (Tehran: N.p., 1962), pp. 35–36.

10. F. Adamiyat, *Asheftegi dar Fekri Tarikhi* (Confusion in historiography) (Tehran: N.p., n.d.), pp. 1–24.

11. R. Khomeini, speech, *Kayhan-e Hava'i*, 28 Dec. 1983.

12. "The Anniversary of Shaykh Nuri's Martyrdom," *Ettela^{C}at*, 2 Aug. 1982.

13. *Ettela^{C}at*, 2 Aug. 1982.

14. E. Browne, *The Persian Revolution* (New York: Barnes and Noble, 1966), p. 444.

15. E. Dillon, "Father and Son—Conservative and Radical: A Gruesome Story," *Contemporary Review* 96 (Oct. 1909): 510–12. Dillon also cooked up a dramatic story of how a Russian revolutionary woman, whom he called the Joan of Arc of the Persian

revolution, had been instrumental in creating bedlam and over-throwing the lawful authorities.

16. M. Malekzadeh, *Tarikh-e Enqelab-e Mashrutiyat-e Iran* (History of the Iranian Constitutional Revolution) (Tehran: Majles Publications, 1943), vol. 6, pp. 132–33.

17. For such a view see J. Madani, *Tarikh-e Siyasi-ye Mo^c aser-e Iran* (The political history of contemporary Iran) (Tehran: Office of Islamic Publication, 1983), vols. 1–2. This was designed as a textbook for the Revolutionary Guards. For an excellent analysis of changing interpretations of the nineteenth-century protests, see M. Afshari, "The Constitutional Movement, Its Historians, and the Making of the Iranian Populist Tradition," *International Journal of Middle East Studies* (forthcoming).

18. On the intellectuals, see F. Adamiyat, *Fekr-e Demokrasi-ye Ejtema^c-ye dar Nahzat-e Mashruteyat-e Iran* (Social Democratic thought in the Constitutional Movement in Iran) (Tehran: Payam Press, 1975). On the merchants, see G. Gilbar, "The Big Merchants and the Persian Revolution of 1906," *Asian and African Studies* 3 (1977): 275–303. On the guilds, see M. Afshari, "The *Pishivaran* and Merchants in Pre-Capitalist Iranian Society," *International Journal of Middle East Studies* 15, no. 2 (May 1983): 133–55. On the liberal aristocrats, see I. Safai, *Rahbaran-e Mashrutiyat* (Leaders of the constitution) (Tehran: Javedan Press, 1973). On the Armenians, see C. Chaqueri, "The Role and Impact of Armenian Intellectuals in Iranian Politics, 1905–1911," *Armenian Review* 41, no. 2 (Summer 1988): 1–51.

19. M. Bayat, *Shi^cism in the Constitutional Revolution of Iran* (New York: Oxford University Press).

20. M. Bamdad, *Tarikh-e Rajal-e Iran* (History of public figures in Iran) (Tehran: Zavar Press, 1968), vol. 3, pp. 96–97.

21. Martin, *Islam and Modernism*, p. 122.

22. V. Martin, "Shaikh Fazlallah Nuri and the Iranian Revolution," *Middle Eastern Studies* 23, no. 1 (1987): 40–41.

23. Ministry of Education, *Tarikh-e Mo^c aser-e Iran* (History of contemporary Iran) (Tehran: Ministry of Education Press, 1984), Year 3, pp. 98–99. None of the primary sources that describe the presiding court mention Yeprem Khan. See Browne,

The Persian Revolution, pp. 444–45; Malekzadeh, *Enqelab-e Mashrutiyat-e Iran*, vol. 6, pp. 118–33; I. Amir-Khizi, *Qiyam-e Azerbayjan va Sattar Khan* (The Azerbayjan Revolt and Sattar Khan) (Tabriz: Shafaq Press, 1950), p. 39. One contemporary source claimed that there was a dramatic confrontation between Shaykh Nuri and Yeprem Khan, who was observing the trial from the public gallery. The same source, however, claims that two months after the execution, Shaykh Nuri's body was as well preserved as the very day he died. See M. Turkoman, *Maktubat, ᶜElamieh-ha, va Chand Gozaresh Peramun-e Naqsheh-e Shaykh Shahid Fazlollah Nuri* (The correspondence, proclamations, and some reports on the mission of the martyred Shaykh Fazlollah Nuri) (Tehran: 1983), vol. 2, pp. 285–316.

24. Khomeini, *Velayat-e Faqih*, p. 12–13.

25. Malekzadeh, *Enqelab-e Mashrutiyat-e Iran*, vol. 2, pp. 19–20; Bayat, *Shiᶜism in the Constitutional Revolution of Iran*, chap. 4; N. Keddie, "Iranian Politics, 1900–1905: Background to Revolution," *Middle Eastern Studies* 5, no. 2 (May 1969): 153.

26. For an unflattering picture of Sattar Khan, see Browne, *The Persian Revolution*, pp. 441–42.

27. British Legation, "Monthly Report for August 1910," PRO, FO 371/Persia 1910/34-950.

28. Safai, *Rahbaran-e Mashrutiyat*, pp. 407–10.

29. Browne, *The Persian Revolution*, pp. 274–75. For a description of the siege and famine, see F. Kazemzadeh, *Russia and Britain in Persia* (New Haven: Yale University Press, 1968), pp. 532–36.

30. H. Katouzian, *The Political Economy of Modern Iran* (New York: New York University Press, 1981), p. 75.

31. S. Ravasani, "How the Gilan Revolution Fell Victim to the Soviet-British Compromise," *Iranshahr* 3, no. 20 (7 Aug. 1981). See also idem, *Nahzat-e Mirza Kuchek Khan Jangali va Avalin Jomhuri-ye Shuravi dar Iran* (The movement of Mirza Kuchek Khan Jangali and the first Soviet Republic of Iran) (Tehran: Tous Press, 1984).

32. H. Jowdat, *Yadbudha-ye Enqelab-e Gilan* (Reminiscences of the Revolution in Gilan) (Tehran: Darakhshan Press, 1972).

33. Madani, *Tarikh-e Siyasi-ye,* vol. 1, pp. 83–86. See also I. Fakhrai, *Sardar-e Jangal* (The forest commander) (Tehran: Javidan Press, 1964).

34. Fakhrai, *Sardar-e Jangal.*

35. M. Donohoe, *With the Persian Expedition* (London: Edward Arnold, 1919), p. 172. This sentiment probably originated during the wartime famine when Kuchek Khan sent food from Gilan to feed the poor of Tehran. See H. Makki, *Modarres: Qahreman-e Azadi* (Modarres: The hero of freedom) (Tehran: Naqsh-e Jahan Press, 1979), vol. 1, p. 147.

36. Donohoe, *Persian Expedition,* p. 72.

37. M. Farrukh, *Khaterat-e Siyasi-ye Farrukh* (Farrukh's political memoirs) (Tehran: Sahami Press, 1969), p. 15.

38. A. Shamideh, "Haydar ^cOmugli," *Donya* 14, no. 1 (1973): 113–24.

39. For the controversy over these negotiations, see *Ayandeh* 9, nos. 2 and 8–9 (1983).

40. For the concept of primitive rebels, see E. Hobsbawm, *Bandits* (New York: Pantheon Books, 1981); and idem, *Primitive Rebels* (New York: Norton, 1959).

41. The Islamic Republic denies that Kuchek Khan received any foreign assistance, but for assistance from the Central Powers, see A. Kasravi, *Tarikh-e Hijdah Saleh-e Azerbayjan* (Eighteen-year history of Azerbayjan) (Tehran: Amir Kaber Press, 1978), p. 813.

42. Ministry of Education, *Tarikh-e Mo^caser-e Iran,* Year 3, p. 131.

43. The British estimated the total forces to be near 1,500. See British Military Attaché to the Foreign Office, "The Situation in Gilan," PRO, FO 371/Persia 1920/34-4907.

44. G. Yeqikian, *Shuravi va Jonbesh-e Jangal* (The Soviets and the Jangali movement) (Tehran: Novin Press, 1984), pp. 324–25.

45. K. Amirzadeh, *Gomnam-e Azadeh* (An obscure freeman) (Tehran: N.p., 1954). See also Yeqikian, *Suravi va Jonbesh-e Jangal,* pp. 137, 230–31, 340–41; and Jowdat, *Yadbudha-ye.*

46. Yeqikian, *Suravi va Jonbesh-e Jangal,* p. 11.

47. Cited in ibid., p. 335.

48. "Kazvin Division Reports," PRO, FO 371/Persia 1920/34-4907.

49. Yeqikian, *Shuravi va Jonbesh-e Jangal*, p. 118.

50. Razvani, *Nahzat-e Mirza Kuchek Khan*.

51. Kuchek Khan, "Message to Mojahedin Brothers," in Yeqikian, *Shuravi va Jonbesh-e Jangal*, pp. 152–60. Fakhrai has reprinted this as "An Unpublished Document from the Forest Commander," *Kayhan-e Farhangi* 20 (Dec. 1985): 20–21.

52. Gauk was a Volga German who had served in the Tsarist legation in Tehran before World War I. During the war, he had been cashiered for misappropriating funds and had been sent to prison in Baku. He joined the Bolsheviks in 1917, returned to Iran with the Red Army in 1920, and soon became Kuchek Khan's translator and close adviser. See Yeqikian, *Shuravi va Jonbesh-e Jangal*, pp. 60, 363–65.

53. Cited by A. Modarresi, "Modarres: A Genius from the Islamic World," *Kayhan-e Farhangi* 26 (Dec. 1985): 24–31.

54. Editor, "Modarres: The Symbol of the Clergy's Struggle against Despotism and Imperialism," *Ettela^{c}at*, 1 Dec. 1982.

55. I. Fakhrai, "The Clergy and Revolution," *Kayhan-e Farhangi* 4, no. 7 (Nov. 1987): 7–11.

56. On the trials of the murderers, see *Parcham*, 25 Oct. 1942.

57. British Legation, "Biographies of Leading Personalities in Persia," PRO, FO 371/Persia 1929/34-9405.

58. Cited by Editor, "The Martyred Ayatollah Sayyid Hasan Modarres: The Great Man of Religion and Politics," *Kayhan-e Farhangi* 4, no. 8 (Nov. 1987): 3. Vol. 2 of M. Bahar, *Tarikh-e Mukhtasar-e Ahzab-e Siyasi-ye Iran* (Short history of Iranian political parties) (Tehran: Amir Kabir Press, 1984), is mostly a record of Modarres's activities in the third through fifth Parliaments.

59. British Legation, "Persian Annual Report for 1925," PRO, FO 371/Persia 1926/34-11500.

60. For Modarres's parliamentary speeches, see H. Makki, *Modarres: Qahreman-e Azadi* (Modarres: The hero of freedom) (Tehran: Naqsh-e Jahan Press, 1984), vols. 1–2.

61. Bahar, *Ahzab-e Siyasi-ye Iran*, vol. 2, pp. 26–27.

62. Editor, "Commemorating the Death of Ayatollah Ka-

shani—The Great Anti-imperialist Crusader," *Ettela^c at*, 14 Mar. 1982. Such biographies ignore completely Kashani's political activities from 1921 until 1941. Some suspected that Kashani received a monthly stipend from Reza Shah throughout his reign. See British Embassy, 24 Jan. 1952, PRO, FO 371/Persia 1952/34-98719.

63. J. Emami, cited by M. Fateh, *Panjah Saleh-e Naft-e Iran* (Fifty years of Iranian oil) (Tehran: Chehr Press, 1956), p. 387.

64. Ministry of Education, *Tarikh-e Mo^c aser-e Iran.*

65. For a summary of National Front criticisms of the Tudeh, see *Karnameh-e Mosaddeq va Hezb-e Tudeh* (Record of Mosaddeq and the Tudeh party) (Florence: Mazda Press, n.d.), vols. 1–2. See also Eman, "From 21 July to 19 August: Mosaddeq Alone," *Showra* 10 (Aug. 1985): 37–59.

66. See Ruhani, *Nahzat-e Imam Khomeini*, vol. 1, p. 230.

67. The debate about the Tudeh officers and the 1953 coup is somewhat unreal. Even if the Tudeh party had mobilized the military network, it would have had little chance of saving Mosaddeq simply because few of its officers held sensitive field posts. Most were doctors, teachers, engineers, and gendarmerie officers. None commanded a militarized division anywhere near the capital. See E. Abrahamian, *Iran between Two Revolutions* (Princeton: Princeton University Press, 1982), p. 338. For a Tudeh account of these crucial days, see N. Kianuri, *Hezb-e Tudeh-e Iran va Doktor Mosaddeq* (The Tudeh party of Iran and Dr. Mosaddeq) (Tehran: Mardom Press, n.d.), pp. 1–15; M. Javanshir, *Tajrabeh-e Best-u-Hasht-e Mordad* (Experience of 19 August) (Tehran: Tudeh Press, 1980). Mosaddeqists reject outright the Tudeh account, but much of it sounds plausible. For a Mosaddeqist rejection, see Katouzian, *The Political Economy of Iran*, pp. 71–72. For a former National Frontist who now accepts the Tudeh account, see E. Mehraban, *Barrasi-ye Mokhtasar-e Ahzab-e Burzhuazi-ye Melli-ye Iran* (Short investigation into Iran's bourgeois political parties) (Tehran: Paik Press, 1980). For a Fatemi colleague who also accepts much of the Tudeh account, see S. Zabih, *The Mossadegh Era* (Chicago: Lake View Press, 1981), pp. 120–21. Zabih is especially helpful because he was able to interview CIA officials.

68. Cited by R. Namvar, "The Issue of Political Trials," *Donya* 7, no. 4 (1966): 43.

69. Ruhani, *Nahzat-e Imam Khomeini*, vol. 1, p. 99.

70. For Kashani's denunciation of the ban, see "The Clergy and the Intellectuals in the Oil Nationalization Campaign," *Ettela^cat-e Haftegi*, 17 Sept. 1987.

71. British Embassy, 14 Nov. 1951, PRO, FO 371/Persia 1951/34-91465.

72. R. Zaehner, 15 May 1952, PRO, FO 248/Persia 1952/34-38572.

73. M. Gasiorowski, "The 1953 Coup D'Etat in Iran," *International Journal of Middle East Studies* 19, no. 3 (Aug. 1987): 263.

74. R. Zaehner, 22 Feb. 1952, PRO, FO 248/Persia 1952/34-38572.

75. Atesh, *Qiyam dar Rah-e Saltanat* (Uprising for the monarchy) (Tehran: N.p, 1954), pp. 50–56.

76. Ayatollah Kashani's press interview is cited by A. Pishdad and H. Katouzian, *Nahzat-e Melli-ye Iran va Doshmanan-e An* (The patriotic movement of Iran and its enemies) (London: National Movement Press, 1981), p. 15.

77. See Iranian Government, *Mozakerat-e Majles-e Showra-ye Melli* (Proceedings of the Consultative National Parliament) (Tehran: Government Publishing House, 1954), 17th Parliament, 4 Jan. 1953, 19 Jan. 1953, 1 Feb. 1953.

78. *Ettela^cat*, 10–13 Nov. 1952.

79. Pishdad and Katouzian, *Nahzat-e Melli-ye Iran*, p. 16.

80. Left Platform, *Fedayan-e Islam* (Los Angeles: N.p., 1985), pp. 222–25. The shah did not crush the Fedayan-e Islam until 1955–56, after it tried to assassinate his prime minister, who had signed the Baghdad Pact.

81. Ibid., p. 16.

82. Cited by Y. Richard, "Ayatollah Kashani: Precursor of the Islamic Republic?" in *Religion and Politics in Iran*, ed. N. Keddie (New Haven: Yale University Press, 1983), p. 121.

83. M. Falsafi, "Fortieth Day of Teacher Motahhari's Martyrdom," *Ettela^cat*, 10 June 1979.

84. A summary of Ayat's attack on Mosaddeq can be found in

F. Rajaee, "Post-revolutionary Historiography in Iran," in *Musaddiq, Iranian Nationalism, and Oil,* ed. J. Bill and W. Louis (Austin: Texas University Press, 1988), pp. 133–36.

85. R. Khomeini, speech, *Kayhan-e Hava'i,* 28 Dec. 1983.

Chapter 5. The Paranoid Style in Iranian Politics

1. R. Hofstadter, *The Paranoid Style in American Politics and Other Essays* (New York: Knopf, 1965).

2. B. Potter, *Plots and Paranoia* (London: Unwin Hyman, 1990). For the notion that the Young Turks were part of a Jewish conspiracy, see D. Fromkin, *A Peace to End All Peace* (New York: Avon Books, 1989).

3. Hofstadter, *The Paranoid Style,* p. 29.

4. G. Curzon, *Persia and the Persian Question* (London: Longmans, 1892), vol. 2, p. 631.

5. A. Lambton, *Islamic Society in Persia* (London: Oxford University Press, 1954), pp. 16–17.

6. H. Vreeland, ed., *Iran* (New Haven: Human Relations Area File, 1957), pp. 4–7.

7. A. Westwood, "The Politics of Distrust in Iran," *Annals of the American Academy of Political and Social Science* 358 (Mar. 1965): 123–35.

8. H. Amirahmadi, *Revolution and Economic Transition: The Iranian Experience* (Albany: State University of New York Press, 1991), pp. 283–84.

9. Vreeland, *Iran,* p. 5.

10. State Department, "Memorandum of the Division of Near Eastern Affairs," *Foreign Relations of the United States* (Washington: U.S. Government Printing Office, 1964), 1943, vol. 4, p. 325.

11. M. Zonis, *The Political Elite of Iran* (Princeton: Princeton University Press, 1971), see esp. pp. 270–71.

12. British Consul, "Bi-weekly Reports," 9 May 1945, PRO, FO 371/Eastern 1945/Persia 222-45476.

13. British Ambassador to the Foreign Office, 9 Feb. 1943, PRO, FO 371/Eastern 1943/Persia 38-35068.

14. British Ambassador to the Foreign Office, 19 Apr. 1943, PRO, FO 371/Eastern 1943/Persia 38-35070.

15. British Ambassador to the Foreign Office, 29 Mar. 1946, PRO, FO 371/Eastern 1946/Persia 34-52670.

16. British Ambassador to the Foreign Office, "The General Situation," PRO, FO 371/Persia 1950/82311.

17. U.S. Ambassador to the State Department, 22 June 1949, *Foreign Relations of the United States*, 1949, vol. 6, p. 529..

18. British Embassy in Tehran, "Paper on the Persian Social and Political Scene," PRO, FO 371/Persia 1951/91460.

19. For an excellent critique of such explanations, see A. Banuazizi, "Iranian 'National Character': A Critique of Some Western Perspectives," in *Psychological Dimensions of Near Eastern Studies*, ed. C. Brown and N. Itzkowitz (Princeton: Darwin Press, 1977), pp. 210–39.

20. Curzon, *Persia and the Persian Question*, vol. 2, p. 623.

21. J. Shaykh al-Islami, "Increase in the Political Influence of Russia and Britain in Iran," *Ettela^{c}at-e Siyasi va Eqtesadi* 35 (Mar.–Apr. 1990): 5.

22. Secretary of State to the U.S. Legation, 11 Feb. 1943, *Foreign Relations of the United States*, 1943, vol. 4, p. 330.

23. A. Lambton, "Some Problems Facing Persia," *International Affairs* 22, no. 2 (Apr. 1946): 254–72.

24. British Ambassador to the Foreign Office, 28 July 1952, PRO, FO 371/Persia 1952/98602; Comments in the Foreign Office, 14 May 1951, PRO, FO 371/Persia 1952/91459; British Embassy to the Foreign Office, 21 May 1951, PRO, FO 371/Persia 1952/91459; British Embassy to the Foreign Office, "Report on Events in Persia in 1951," PRO, FO 371/Persia 1951/98593; Foreign Office to the British Ambassador to the U.N., PRO, FO 371/Persia 1951/91606.

25. British Embassy to the Foreign Office, 28 July 1952, PRO, FO 371/Persia 1952/98602.

26. British Ambassador to the Foreign Office, 21 May 1951, PRO, FO 371/Persia 1951/91459.

27. British Embassy to the Foreign Office, "A Comparison be-

tween Persian and Asian Nationalisms in General," PRO, FO 371/
Persia 1951/91464.

28. Special Correspondent, "Persia's Present Leaders,"
Times, 22 Aug. 1951, filed in PRO, FO 248/Persia 1951/1514.

29. "Mohammad Moussadek," *Observer*, 20 May 1951, filed
in ibid.

30. Information Policy Department of the Foreign Office, 4
Sept. 1951, PRO, FO 2481/Persia 1951/1528.

31. British Embassy in Washington to the Foreign Office, 11
July 1951, PRO, FO 371/Persia 1951/1528.

32. E. Berthoud, "Persian-Oil Dispute: The Views of Miss
Lambton," PRO, FO 371/Persia 1951/91609.

33. British Embassy to the War Office, 4 Aug. 1952, PRO, FO
371/Persia 1952/98602.

34. For a typical report on his activities, see R. Zaehner, secret
memo, 15 May 1952, PRO, FO 248/Persia 1952/1531.

35. Notes made in London, 22 Apr. 1952, PRO, FO 371/Persia
1952/98599.

36. See A. Alam, *The Shah and I* (New York: St. Martin's
Press, 1991), pp. 443, 497. See also D. Wilber, *Adventures in the
Middle East* (Princeton: Darwin Press, 1986), p. 148.

37. Khomeini, *Velayat-e Faqih*, pp. 7, 41–42, 179.

38. R. Khomeini, speech, *Ettela^Cat*, 13 Jan. 1980.

39. Khomeini, *Velayat-e Faqih*, p. 179.

40. Ibid., pp. 11–12.

41. Ibid., pp. 17, 179; R. Khomeini, speech, *Ettela^Cat*, 21 May
1979, 12 Jan. 1980, 13 Jan. 1980.

42. Front for the Liberation of the Iranian People, *Khomeini
va Jonbesh*, pp. 20–21.

43. Ibid.

44. R. Khomeini, speech, *Kayhan-e Hava'i*, 27 July 1988.

45. R. Khomeini, speech, *Kayhan-e Hava'i*, 5 Sept. 1984.

46. R. Khomeini, speech, *Ettela^Cat*, 26 Sept. 1979, 23 March
1980.

47. R. Khomeini, speech, *Ettela^Cat*, 21 June 1979.

48. R. Khomeini, speech, *Ettela^Cat*, 26 June 1980.

49. Ibid.

50. R. Khomeini, speech, *Kayhan-e Hava'i*, 27 July 1988.

51. R. Khomeini, speech on the political role of the clergy, in *Islamic Unity against Imperialism: Eight Documents of the Islamic Revolution in Iran* (New York: Islamic Association of Iranian Professionals and Merchants in America, 1981), p. 8.

52. Khomeini, *Velayat-e Faqih*, pp. 6–7; Ruhani, *Nahzat-e Imam Khomeini*, vol. 1, pp. 316, 459, 656; vol. 2, pp. 700–701.

53. Khomeini, *Velayat-e Faqih*, p. 175.

54. R. Khomeini, speech, *Ettela^Cat*, 29 May 1983.

55. Ruhani, *Nahzat-e Imam Khomeini*, vol. 2, p. 237. In actual fact, it is verse 50.

56. Ibid., vol. 1, p. 318.

57. Ibid., pp. 598, 607–8.

58. A. Khamanei, Friday sermon, *Kayhan-e Hava'i*, 11 Apr. 1990.

59. "Bahaism," *Kayhan-e Hava'i*, 1 Nov. 1989.

60. S. Vahadi, "Kasravi: Reza Khan's Cultural Theoretician," *Ettela^Cat*, 29 Jan. 1984.

61. M. Naqavi, "Islam and Nationalism," *Ettela^Cat*, 7 Dec. 1983.

62. Ministry of Education, *Tarikh-e Mo^Caser-e Iran*, Year 3, pp. 37–38.

63. *Iran Times*, 7 Dec. 1990.

64. "Imperialism in History," *Kayhan-e Hava'i*, 30 Dec. 1987–16 Nov. 1988.

65. H. Malek, *Nabard-e Pruzheh-ha-ye Siyasi dar Sahneh-e Iran* (The struggles of political projects in the Iranian scene) (N.p., 1982).

66. Such attitudes overflow into the academic world. For example, Feraydun Adamiyat, a Mosaddeqist and the leading Iranian historian of the Constitutional Revolution, argues that Nikki Keddie, the leading American historian of the same revolution, systematically exaggerated the role of the clergy in nineteenth-century politics because she is Jewish and her research was funded by the Guggenheim Foundation. See F. Adamiyat, *Ideolozhi-ye Nahzat-e Mashrutiyat-e Iran* (The ideology of the Iranian constitutional movement) (Tehran: Payam Press, 1976), p. 33;

idem, *Shuresh bar Emtiyaznameh-ye Rezhi* (Revolt against the tobacco concession) (Tehran: Payam Press, 1981), p. 146.

67. R. Mehrban, *Gusheh-ha-ye az Tarikh-e Mo^{c}aser-e Iran* (Pieces from the history of contemporary Iran) (N.p.: ^{c}Atard Press, 1982).

68. Toilers' Party, *Afsaneh-ha-ye Hezb-e Tudeh* (The Tudeh party myths) (Tehran: Toilers' Party Press, 1952).

69. For discussion of these forgeries, see PRO, FO 371/Persia 1951/91593.

70. American Embassy to the State Department, "The Tudeh Party Today (October 1952)," *The Declassified Documentation Retrospective Collection: 1952–4 (75)308D* (Washington, D.C.: U.S. Government Printing Office).

71. State Department, "Leaders and Members of the Tudeh Party," *OSS/State Department—Intelligence and Research Reports, Part XII: The Middle East: 1950–1961 Supplement* (Washington, D.C.: U.S. Government Printing Office).

72. M. Pahlavi, *Answer to History* (New York: Scarborough Press, 1982), p. 73.

73. Ibid., p. 59.

74. Ibid., pp. 70–71. In actual fact, Mosaddeq had agreed to form a cabinet on condition he could hold a referendum to reform the electoral law, which deprived illiterates of the vote. He hoped thereby to diminish the influence of the landed upper class. See British Ambassador to the Foreign Office, 22 Jan. 1944, PRO, FO 371/Persia 1944/40186. At the time, the British ambassador described Mosaddeq as an "epileptic" "windbag" who was "touchy" and overly "nationalistic." See British Ambassador to the Foreign Office, 20 Jan. 1944, in ibid.

75. Pahlavi, *Answer to History*, p. 171.

76. Ibid., pp. 103–4.

77. Ibid., pp. 96–97.

78. Ibid., p. 155.

79. Ibid., p. 145.

80. Military Governor of Tehran, *Evolution of Communism in Iran* (Tehran: Kayhan Press, 1959).

81. W. Butler, "Memorandum to the International Commission of Jurists on Private Audience with the Shah (30 May 1977)" (unpublished).

82. *The Betrayal of Iran* (N.p., 1979), pp. 1–89.

83. Alam, *The Shah and I*, pp. 89, 122, 169, 239, 341, and 381.

84. H. Fardoust, "Television Interviews," *Kayhan-e Hava'i*, 30 Nov. 1988–25 Jan. 1989.

85. H. Fardoust, "Memoirs," *Kayhan-e Hava'i*, 1 July–23 Oct. 1991.

Epilogue

1. The term *khatt-e imam* (imam's line), which was used throughout the Islamic Revolution, has a Stalinist genealogy. Religious radicals had borrowed the term "line" from the Confederation of Iranian Students in Exile, which had taken it from Mao Tse-tung's Cultural Revolution. Mao Tse-tung, of course, had taken it from the Soviet Union. Thus Stalin's line of the Party became the line of the imam.

2. A. Meshkini, speech, *Kayhan*, 19 June 1989.

3. A. Rafsanjani, Friday sermon, *Kayhan-e Hava'i*, 14 June 1989.

4. A. Rafsanjani, Friday sermon, *Kayhan*, 4 Nov. 1989.

5. *Salam*, 5 Apr. 1992.

6. *Resalat*, 30 Apr. 1992.

7. *Resalat*, 29 Apr. 1992.

8. *Resalat*, 14 Mar. 1992.

9. *Resalat*, 2 Oct. 1991.

10. *Resalat*, 26 Feb. 1990.

11. *Resalat*, 26 Feb. 1992.

12. Q. Shu^cleh-Saedi, parliamentary speech, *Resalat*, 9 Dec. 1991.

13. *Kayhan*, 14 Jan. 1992.

14. A. Rafsanjani, Friday sermon, *Kayhan-e Hava'i*, 22 Apr. 1992.

15. A. Rafsanjani, Friday sermon, *Kayhan*, 12 Aug. 1991.

16. *New York Times*, 10 Apr. 1992.

17. A. Khamenei, Friday sermon, *Kayhan-e Hava'i*, 11 Oct. 1989.

18. A. Rafsanjani, speech, *Kayhan*, 17 July 1991.

19. For parliamentary speeches, see *Resalat*, Apr. 1991–June 1992.

Glossary

ayatollah (lit. God's symbol). Modern term for a high-ranking cleric.

bazaar. Marketplace.

bazaari. The people of the marketplace.

chador. Full-length veil.

Cossacks. A brigade created by Tsarist officers.

ejtehad. Seminary degree.

elteqati. Eclectic.

enqelab. Revolution.

^cerfan. Mysticism, gnostic knowledge.

faqih (pl. *fuqaha*). Religious jurist.

fatwa. Decree.

fiqh. Religious jurisprudence.

hadith. Tradition relating to the Prophet and his companions.

hezbollahis. Members of the Party of God.

hojjat al-Islam. Middle-ranking clerics.

imam. Leader.

kafer. Unbelievers, infidels.

khoms. Religious taxes.

marja^c-e taqlid (pl. *maraje^c-e taqlid*) (lit. source of emulation). A cleric of the highest rank.

mojahed (pl. *mojahedin*). Freedom fighter, crusader.

mojtahed. Senior cleric.

mostakberin. Oppressors, exploiters.

mostazafin. The oppressed, the exploited, and the meek.

qeshr. Stratum.

rahbar. Leader.

shahid. Martyr.

shari^c a. Sacred law.

sotun-e panjom. Fifth columnists.

tabaqeh (pl. *tabaqat*). Class.

ulama. Clergy.

velayat-e faqih. Jurist's guardianship.

Select Bibliography
on Khomeini

Abrahamian, E. *The Iranian Mojahedin.* New Haven: Yale University Press, 1989.

Akhavan-Tawhidi, H. [pseud.] *Dar Pas-e Pardeh-e Tazvir* (Behind the veils of dissimulation). Paris: N.p., 1984.

Akhavi, S. *Religion and Politics in Contemporary Iran.* Albany: State University of New York Press, 1980.

———. "The Ideology and Praxis of Shi^{c}ism in the Iranian Revolution." *Comparative Studies in Society and History* 25, no. 2 (Apr. 1983): 195–221.

———. "Islam, Politics and Society in the Thought of Ayatullah Khomeini, Ayatullah Taliqani and Ali Shariati." *Middle Eastern Studies* 24, no. 4 (Oct. 1988): 404–31.

———. "Shiism, Corporatism, and Rentierism in the Iranian Revolution." In *Comparative Muslim Societies,* ed. J. Cole, pp. 261–94. Ann Arbor: University of Michigan Press, 1992.

Algar, H. *Islam and Revolution: Writings and Declarations of Imam Khomeini.* Berkeley: Mizan Press, 1981.

Arjomand, S. "The State and Khomeini's Islamic Order." *Iranian Studies* 13, nos. 1–4 (1980): 147–64.

———. *The Turban for the Crown: The Islamic Revolution in Iran.* New York: Oxford University Press, 1988.

———, ed. *From Nationalism to Revolutionary Islam.* Albany: State University of New York Press, 1984.

———, ed. *Authority and Political Culture in Shi^{c}ism.* Albany: State University of New York Press, 1988.

Ashtiyani, A. "Revival of Religious Thought and the Perplexity of

Political Islam in the Iranian Revolution." *Kankash* 5 (Autumn 1989): 51–85.

Bakhash, S. *The Reign of the Ayatollahs.* New York: Basic Books, 1984.

———. "Islam and Social Justice in Iran." In *Shi^Cism, Resistance, and Revolution,* ed. M. Kramer, pp. 95–115. Boulder: Westview Press, 1987.

———. "The Politics of Land, Law, and Social Justice in Iran." *Middle East Journal* 43, no. 2 (Spring 1989): 186–201.

Banuazizi, A., and M. Weiner, eds. *The State, Religion, and Ethnic Politics.* Syracuse: Syracuse University Press, 1986.

Bayat, G. "The Iranian Revolution of 1979: Fundamentalist or Modern?" *Middle East Journal* 37, no. 1 (Winter 1983): 30–42.

———. "Taleqani and the Iranian Revolution." In *Shi^Cism, Resistance, and Revolution,* ed. M. Kramer, pp. 67–93. Boulder: Westview Press, 1987.

Behrooz, M. "Factionalism in Iran under Khomeini." *Middle Eastern Studies* 27, no. 4 (Oct. 1991): 597–614.

Bill, J. "Power and Religion in Revolutionary Iran." *Middle East Journal* 36, no. 1 (Winter 1982): 22–47.

Burrell, R. *Islamic Fundamentalism.* London: Royal Asiatic Society, 1989.

Busheri, M. "The Early Years of Ruhollah Mosavi Khomeini." *Cheshmandaz* 5 (Autumn 1988): 12–37.

———. "From *Secrets Unveiled* to *Thousand Year Secrets.*" *Cheshmandaz* 6 (Summer 1989): 14–26.

Calder, N. "Accommodation and Revolution in Imami Shi^Ci Jurisprudence." *Middle Eastern Studies* 18, no. 1 (Jan. 1982): 1–20.

Choueri, Y. *Islamic Fundamentalism.* Boston: G. K. Hall, 1990.

Cohen, N., ed. *The Fundamentalist Phenomenon.* Grand Rapids, Mich.: Eerdmans Publishing, 1990.

Cole, J., and N. Keddie, eds. *Shi^Cism and Social Protest.* New Haven: Yale University Press, 1986.

Davani, A. *Nahzat-e Ruhaniyun-e Iran* (The movement of the Iranian clergy). 10 vols. Qom: Imam Reza Foundation, 1981.

Eliash, J. "Misconceptions regarding the Juridical Status of the

Iranian Ulama." *International Journal of Middle East Studies* 10, no. 1 (Feb. 1979): 9–25.

Enayat, H. *Modern Islamic Political Thought.* London: Macmillan, 1982.

———. "Iran: Khumayni's Concept of the 'Guardianship of the Juristconsult.' " In *Islam in the Political Process*, ed. J. Piscatori, pp. 160–80. New York: Cambridge University Press, 1983.

Esposito, J., ed. *The Iranian Revolution: Its Global Impact.* Miami: Florida International University Press, 1990.

Ferdows, A. "Khomaini and Fedayan's Society and Politics." *International Journal of Middle East Studies* 15, no. 2 (May 1983): 241–57.

Fischer, M. *Iran: From Religious Dispute to Revolution.* Cambridge: Harvard University Press, 1980.

———. "Islam and the Revolt of the Petit Bourgeoisie." *Daedalus* 111, no. 2 (Winter 1982): 101–23.

———. "Imam Khomeini: Four Levels of Understanding." In *Voices of Resurgent Islam*, ed. J. Esposito, pp. 150–74. New York: Oxford University Press, 1983.

Front for the Liberation of the Iranian People (JAMA). *Khomeini va Jonbesh* (Khomeini and the movement). N.p.: Moharram Press, 1973.

———. *Majmu^{c}eh az Maktubat, Sukhanrani-ha, Payham-ha, va Raftari-ha-ye Imam Khomeini* (Collection from Imam Khomeini's teachings, speeches, messages, and activities). Tehran: Chapkhesh Press, n.d.

Haghayeghi, M. "Agrarian Reform Problems in Post-revolutionary Iran." *Middle Eastern Studies* 26, no. 1 (Jan. 1990): 35–51.

Hairi, A. "The Legacy of the Early Qajar Rule as Viewed by the Shi^{c}i Religious Leaders." *Middle Eastern Studies* 24, no. 3 (July 1988): 271–86.

Halliday, F. "The Iranian Revolution: Uneven Development and Religious Populism." In *State and Ideology in the Middle East and Pakistan*, ed. F. Halliday and H. Alavi, pp. 31–64. New York: Monthly Review Press, 1988.

Hooglund, E. "Rural Iran and the Clerics." *Merip* 104 (Mar.–Apr. 1982): 23–26.

———. "Social Origins of the Revolutionary Clergy." In *The Iranian Revolution and the Islamic Republic*, ed. N. Keddie and E. Hooglund, pp. 74–90. Syracuse: Syracuse University Press, 1986.

Kaplan, L., ed. *Fundamentalism in Comparative Perspective.* Amherst: University of Massachusetts Press, 1992.

Kazemi, F., ed. *Iranian Revolution in Perspective.* Special issue of *Iranian Studies* 13, nos. 1–4 (1980).

Keddie, N. *Roots of Revolution.* New Haven: Yale University Press, 1981.

———. *Religion and Politics in Iran.* New Haven: Yale University Press, 1983.

Khavari, M. "Khomeinism and the Historical Development of Shiism." *Akhtar* 1 (Spring 1984): 3–43.

Khomeini, R. *Kashf al-Asrar* (Secrets unveiled). Tehran: N.p., 1943.

———. *Velayat-e Faqih: Hokumat-e Islami* (The jurist's guardianship: Islamic government). Tehran: N.p., 1978.

———. *Towzih al-Masa'el* (Questions clarified). Tehran: N.p., 1978.

———. *Matn-e Kamel-e Vasiyatnameh-e Elahi va Siyasi-ye Imam Khomeini* (The complete text of Imam Khomeini's divine will and political testament). *Kayhan-e Hava'i*, 14 June 1989.

Kimmel, M., ed. *Religion and Revolution in Iranian Society.* Special issue of *Social Compass* 36, no. 4 (Dec. 1989).

Lambton, A. "A Reconsideration of the Position of the Marja[c] al-Taqlid." *Studia Islamica* 20 (1964): 115–35.

Left Platform. *Fedayan-e Islam.* Los Angeles: N.p., 1985.

Loeffler, L. *Islam in Practice.* Albany: State University of New York Press, 1988.

McEoin, D. "Aspects of Militancy and Quietism in Imami Shi[c]ism." *Bulletin of the British Society of Middle East Studies* 11, no. 1 (1984): 18–27.

Menashri, D. "Shi[c]i Leadership." *Iranian Studies* 13, nos. 1–4 (1980): 119–46.

Ministry of Islamic Guidance. *Sahifah-e Nur: Majmu^{c}eh Rahna-vard-ha-ye Imam Khomeini* (Leaves of illumination: Collection of Imam Khomeini's messages). 17 vols. Tehran: Ministry of Guidance Press, 1981–89.

Moaddel, M. "The Shi^{c}i Ulama and the State in Iran." *Theory and Society* 15 (1986): 519–56.

———. "Ideology as Episodic Discourse: The Case of the Iranian Revolution." *American Sociological Review* 57 (June 1992): 353–79.

Mottahedeh, R. "Iran's Foreign Devils." *Foreign Policy* 38 (Spring 1980): 19–34.

———. *The Mantle of the Prophet.* New York: Simon and Schuster, 1985.

Moussavi, A. "A New Interpretation of the Theory of *Velayat-e Faqih.*" *Middle Eastern Studies* 28, no. 1 (Jan. 1992): 101–7.

Pakdaman, N. "Until the Death of Khomeinism." *Cheshmandaz* 6 (Summer 1989): 1–13.

———. "The End of the Jurist's Guardianship." *Cheshmandaz* 7 (Spring 1990): 1–21.

Pasandideh, M. "The Life of the Leader of the Revolution." *Iran Times,* 17 Mar.–19 May 1989.

Paya, A. "The Jurist's Absolute Guardianship." *Cheshmandaz* 4 (Spring 1988): 15–49.

Piscatori, J., ed. *Islamic Fundamentalism and the Gulf Crisis.* Chicago: American Academy of Arts and Sciences, 1991.

Rahnema, A., and F. Nomani. *The Secular Miracle.* London: Zed Press, 1990.

Rajaee, F. *Islamic Values and World View: Khomeyni on Man, the State and International Politics.* New York: University Press of America, 1983.

Ruhani, H. *Nahzat-e Imam Khomeini* (Imam Khomeini's movement). 2 vols. Tehran: Iman's Way Press, 1984.

Savory, R. "Ex Oriente Nebula." In *Ideology and Power in the Middle East,* ed. P. Chelkowski and R. Pranger, pp. 339–64. Durham, N.C.: Duke University Press, 1988.

Sivan, E. "Sunni Radicalism in the Middle East and the Iranian Revolution." *International Journal of Middle East Studies* 21, no. 1 (Feb. 1989): 1–30.

"Special Issue on Populism in Developing Countries." *Nezam-e Novin* 4 (Spring 1981): 1–231.

Stowasser, B., ed. *The Islamic Impulse.* Washington, D.C.: Croom Helm, 1987.

Taheri, A. *The Spirit of Allah.* Bethesda: Adler and Alder, 1986.

Tehran University Publication Center. *Mosahebeh-ha-ye Imam Khomeini dar Najaf, Paris, va Qom* (Imam Khomeini's interviews in Najaf, Paris, and Qom). Tehran: Tehran University Press, 1981.

Vajdani, M., ed. *Sarguzashtha-ye Vezhah az Zindegani-e Hazrat Imam Khomeini* (Special reminiscences from the life of His Excellency Imam Khomeini). 6 vols. Tehran: Payam-e Azadi Press, 1982–89.

Wright, M., ed. *Iran: The Khomeini Revolution.* London: Longman, 1989.

Wright, R. *Sacred Rage: The Wrath of Militant Islam.* New York: Simon and Schuster, 1985.

———. *In the Name of God: The Khomeini Decade.* New York: Simon and Schuster, 1989.

Zonis, M., and D. Brumberg. *Khomeini, the Islamic Republic of Iran, and the Arab World.* Cambridge: Harvard Middle East Center, 1987.

Zubaida, S. "The Quest for the Islamic State." *Studies in Religious Fundamentalism,* ed. L. Caplan, pp. 25–50. Albany: State University of New York Press, 1987.

———. "An Islamic State: The Case of Iran." *Merip* 153 (July–Aug. 1988): 3–7.

———. *Islam, the People and the State.* London: Routledge, 1989.

Index

CPSIA information can be obtained
at www.ICGtesting.com
Printed in the USA
JSHW031939180620
6261JS00001B/50